D0765699

NATIONAL UNIVERSITY LIBRARY

044870

SEPARATION ANXIETY DISORDER
Psychodynamics and Psychotherapy

RICHARD A. GARDNER, M.D.

Clinical Professor of Child Psychiatry
Columbia University, College of Physicians and Surgeons

Creative Therapeutics
155 County Road
Cresskill, New Jersey 07626

© 1985 by Creative Therapeutics, 155 County Road, Cresskill, New Jersey 07626

All rights reserved. No part of this book may be reproduced in any form or by any means without permission in writing from the publisher.

PRINTED IN THE UNITED STATES OF AMERICA

10   9   8   7   6   5   4   3   2   1

Library of Congress Cataloging in Publication Data

Gardner, Richard A.
   Separation anxiety disorder.

   Bibliography: p. 177
   1. Separation anxiety in children.   2. Child
psychotherapy.   I. Title.   [DNLM: 1. Anxiety, Separation—
therapy.   2. Psychotherapy.   WM 172 G228s]
RJ506.S46G37   1985   618.92′85223   84–26348
ISBN 0–933812–10–8

To my children

Andrew Kevin

Nancy Tara

and

Julie Anne

for providing me with pride
and joy beyond expectations

Contents

Acknowledgments

I am deeply indebted to my ever faithful secretary Mrs. Linda Gould for her dedication to the task of typing the manuscript of this book. The typing assistance by Mrs. Carol Gibbon, Mrs. Catherine Watkins, and Mrs. Helen Bleecker is also appreciated. All worked with serious dedication and provided me with an accurate and highly presentable manuscript.

This is the first of my books in which the original manuscript was typed with my word processor. I am indebted to my son Andrew Gardner for his encouraging my original purchase of this instrument and his guidance on the long road to mastering its complexities. Its utilization facilitated immensely the typing and editing of the manuscript.

Once again, Mrs. Barbara Christenberry dedicated herself to the editing of the manuscript. She achieved well that delicate balance between firm criticism and flexibility to my wishes that are crucial to the good editor-author relationship. I feel fortunate for having had her assistance. The assistance of Mrs. Frances Dubner in the editing of the manuscript is also deeply appreciated. Especially valuable were her contributions that stemmed from her experiences as a teacher.

Other Books by Richard A. Gardner

The Boys and Girls Book About Divorce
Therapeutic Communication with Children:
    The Mutual Storytelling Technique
Dr. Gardner's Stories About the Real World, Volume I
Dr. Gardner's Stories About the Real World, Volume II
Dr. Gardner's Fairy Tales for Today's Children
Understanding Children—A Parents Guide to Child Rearing
MBD: The Family Book About Minimal Brain Dysfunction
Psychotherapeutic Approaches to the Resistant Child
Psychotherapy with Children of Divorce
Dr. Gardner's Modern Fairy Tales
The Parents Book About Divorce
The Boys and Girls Book About One-Parent Families
The Objective Diagnosis of Minimal Brain Dysfunction
Dorothy and the Lizard of Oz
Dr. Gardner's Fables for Our Times
The Boys and Girls Book About Stepfamilies
Family Evaluation in Child Custody Litigation

Introduction

The separation anxiety disorder is one of the "purer" clinical entities in child psychiatry. When seen in its full-blown form it is hard to miss the diagnosis. There are few diagnoses in all of psychiatry in which there is greater inter-rater reliability than the separation anxiety disorder. Not only does the purity of the disorder contribute to the ease with which it is diagnosed, but the psychodynamic processes that are often contributory also have a uniformity and consistency that is unusual in psychiatric disorders. All psychogenic disorders are multidetermined, but the variation among individuals with regard to the specific psychodynamic factors that contribute to the symptoms is formidable. Although there are certainly variations with regard to these contributing factors in the separation anxiety disorder, most examiners agree that there is far less variability in the clinical picture, family contributions, and psychodynamic patterns in this form of psychopathology. Of course, like all other forms of psychiatric disturbance, the separation anxiety disorder may exist in milder forms and may thereby be less readily recognized.

Because of its relative purity, the therapeutic approaches to this disturbance are also more readily standardized. Like other childhood disorders, the facility with which it can be treated varies. Some cases can be dealt with quite easily, but in others the pathology is deep-seated and the family contributions are so formidable that they may be impossible to treat successfully. In this book I shall describe in detail the psychodynamic patterns that I have found to be most consistently present and the psychotherapeutic approaches that I have found to be most efficacious.

In recent years we have seen in psychiatry a swing of the pendulum back to a biological orientation when explaining the etiology of a wide variety of psychiatric disturbances. Under the influence of psychoanalysis, from the 1940s to the 1960s many disorders that we would now consider to be organic in etiology were viewed as being psychogenic. I believe, however, that the pendulum has swung too far and that many purely psychogenic disorders are being viewed as being physiologic or neurologic in etiology. And this has been the case for the separation anxiety disorder in that there are some examiners who hold that it is a biological disturbance which needs only be treated by medication. I am in full disagreement with this opinion. I believe that the separation anxiety disorder is psychogenic in etiology and that medication should play only a limited role in its treatment. Accordingly, this book will deal primarily with the disorder's psychodynamics and psychotherapy, with only limited space devoted to a discussion of the role of drugs.

At this point, clarification of the terms *fear, anxiety,* and *phobia* is warranted. The term *fear* is generally used when there is a specific entity that is the focus of the fear. In a small child fear of a big dog, thunder, and "scary" rides in the amusement park are understandable and do not necessarily indicate the presence of neurotic mechanisms. An adult's fear when a shark's fin is seen in the water or when the earth begins to tremble is certainly warranted. Fear has both psychological and physiological aspects. The psychological includes the affective and the cognitive components, the feelings and thoughts that are evoked by a realistic danger. The physiological components include rapid heart and pulse rates, increased respiratory rate, the shunting of blood to the brain and skeletal muscles and away from the gastrointestinal tract. The fear reaction serves a purpose: It enhances one's efficiency in removing oneself from a danger. It is reasonable to assume that individuals with slowly arising or weak fear reactions did not survive as well over the course of evolution as did those with quicker and stronger fear reactions. In a sense, fear is the opposite of anger. When confronted with a danger we can either fight or flee. Both have survival value. The term fear is warranted when it is the general consensus of observers that the individual is justified in experiencing the response and that the danger is real.

In *phobia* the same physiological reactions are operative, namely, the increased heart rate, respiratory rate, and so on. However, there is a difference with regard to the psychological mechanisms. Emotionally, there is the same feeling of fear and the individual's mentation is also one relating to the danger and impending harm. However, the main difference between the *phobia* and the *fear* is that in the phobia the general consensus of observers is that the fright reaction is either totally inappropriate or grossly exaggerated. In the fear reaction the flight reaction is generally considered to be warranted. The phobic object may be one that the vast majority of people are not afraid of—for example, an open area (agoraphobia) or crowded or closed places (claustrophobia). There may be an exaggerated fear. On rare occasions the normal person may fear that a fire may break out in a theater. People with phobias are so obsessed with the fear that they will be caught in such a fire that they may be either unable to attend a theater or only able to attend when seated next to an emergency exit. The phobia, then, is a pathological fear and usually involves the utilization of neurotic mechanisms such as displacement (displacing the fear from what is really feared to something that is not the real source), avoidance (utilizing the fear for the purpose of avoiding an unpleasant situation), projection (projecting a feeling like anger and then avoiding it fearfully in order to deny the anger within oneself), and symbolism (fearing something that symbolizes another entity).

Anxiety also involves the same physiological reactions as fear and phobia. However, in anxiety the individual does not have a specific mental representation of the feared object. The individual is often at a loss to know why the fearful reaction is taking place. The pounding heart may result in the individual's fearing that he or she may die. This is a secondary phenomenon. Many psychoanalysts hold that anxiety is the result of the threatened eruption into conscious awareness of unconscious thoughts and feelings about which the individual feels guilty. For example, the individual may suppress and repress sexual or angry feelings because of guilt. When these build up and threaten eruption into conscious awareness, the anxiety serves as a signal that "dangerous" thoughts and/or feelings are emerging into conscious awareness. Although an analyst myself, I do not believe that the traditional analytical explanation holds for many of the patients I see who exhibit anxiety and panic states. I believe that there are a wide range of individuals with regard to the sensitivity of the fear reaction. Some individuals have a high threshold and others a very low threshold. Those with a low threshold may have their fear mechanisms triggered by innocuous or minimal stimuli, sometimes stimuli that are unrecognized by the patient. In some cases there may be no external stimulus at all; rather, the mechanisms are brought into play in a manner similar to a seizure. Here there are basically biochemical, neurophysiological, and metabolic mechanisms that are operative, and this disorder can truly be viewed as a purely biological entity in these patients. In others the psychoanalytic explanation appears reasonable.

In 1941, Johnson *et al.* introduced the term *school phobia* (Gordon and Young, 1976). The term appeared warranted because the child's fear of school was clearly neurotic and far beyond any realistic danger that the child could describe. Prior to that time, school phobia was not generally recognized as a discreet disorder. Rather, it was included among other school problems, especially those involving refusal and truancy. The term school phobia has applicability because the child will focus on the school as the source of the fear. In addition, because it is not really the school the child is basically afraid of, the distortion warrants the utilization of the term phobia. In some cases the child is less certain about the exact nature of the fear. The child may resist going to school, but cannot say exactly what it is in the school situation that causes the fear. The child does not present with the usual array of rationalizations for not attending (to be discussed below) and does not delineate specific factors in the school that he or she is afraid of. There is, however, a morbid sense of fear as the child approaches the schoolhouse. This nonspecific fear is more justifiably called anxiety. In 1957, Johnson suggested that the term "school phobia" was a misnomer in that the basic fear was not that of the school but that of separation from the mother and that "the essential problem lay in an unresolved, mutual dependency relationship between mother and child" (Skynner and Robin, 1976). The child is not consciously aware of the fact that the basic fear relates to separation from the mother and a variety of other factors that will be discussed below. Psychoanalytic theory holds that anxiety results from the threat that these unconscious thoughts and feelings will erupt into conscious awareness. The school situation increases the likelihood of such eruption, and the anxiety is related to this threat.

Because of these considerations, the term *separation anxiety disorder* has been substituted for school phobia. And this is the term used in DSM-III (1980). Because the school is the conscious fear object for these children, I do not believe it is justifiable to discard the term *school phobia* entirely. We have not discarded the term *agoraphobia* with the argument that for agoraphobics the fear of open places is merely a displacement and is symbolic of factors having little to do with open places. Similarly, we have not disbanded the term *claustrophobia* with the argument that people who fear closed places really fear something else. Accordingly, in my discussion, I will occasionally use the term *school phobia,* and otherwise use the term *separation anxiety disorder.* I prefer to retain the original term because there are situations in which it appears to be the more applicable, that is, when the child focuses specifically on the school. I will also use the term separation anxiety disorder because there are children who do not focus on the school and the primary symptomatic manifestation is diffuse anxiety. Some children will state that they fear that something "bad" (not necessarily defined) will happen to their mothers while they are in school. Here the separation anxiety element is apparent and the psychodynamic significance of this particular response will be discussed in detail in Chapter Three. In some cases, of course, it is unclear as to which term is warranted. Accordingly, I shall use the terms *fear, phobia,* and *anxiety* when referring to these children. Physiologically, however, they are identical. It is the cognitive and emotional concomitants that determine which of the terms is the most appropriate.

The *Diagnostic and Statistical Manual of Mental Disorders* (DSM-III) (1980) uses the term *separation anxiety disorder.* The manual states that in order to justify the diagnosis at least three of the following diagnostic criteria must be satisfied:

1. unrealistic worry about possible harm befalling major attachment figures or fear that they will leave and will not return
2. unrealistic worry that an untoward calamitous event will separate the child from a major attachment figure, e.g., the child will be lost, kidnapped, killed, or be the victim of an accident

3. persistent reluctance or refusal to go to school in order to stay with major attachment figures or at home
4. persistent reluctance or refusal to go to sleep without being next to a major attachment figure or to go to sleep away from home
5. persistent avoidance of being alone in the home and emotional upset if unable to follow the major attachment figure around the home
6. repeated nightmares involving theme of separation
7. complaints of physical symptoms on school days, e.g., stomachaches, headaches, nausea, vomiting
8. signs of excessive distress upon separation, or when anticipating separation, from major attachment figures, e.g., temper tantrums or crying, pleading with parents not to leave (for children below the age of six, the distress must be of panic proportions)
9. social withdrawal, apathy, sadness or difficulty concentrating on work or play when not with a major attachment figure

I consider it to be of interest that the word "school" is not mentioned until one reaches criterion # 3 and that mention is made of school in only one of the other nine criteria categories (# 7). Apparently, the committee wished to deemphasize the school situation and emphasize the fact that school anxiety is only one part of a larger clinical picture. I am in disagreement with the committee's deemphasis here. I believe that the fear of going to school is the predominant symptom. It is not only the child's major source of distress, but is the one that attracts the most attention. The panic attacks are severest in the school where the child's shrieking may literally interfere with teachers' conducting their routines. Complaints from significant figures are greatest over this symptom, both from the school and often by parents (the mother's ambivalence notwithstanding). This is not surprising considering the fact that the law requires the child to go to school and in the schoolroom the child feels trapped. It is for these reasons that I depart from the DSM-III description and consider the school fear to be the primary symptomatic manifestation and consider the other fears as associated features.

1

The Typical Clinical Picture

PRIMARY MANIFESTATIONS

Clinically, the picture that one sees appears to justify the original term *school phobia*. The most salient feature is fear of going to school to the point of panic. The closer the child gets to the school the greater the fear. However, if the mother accompanies the child into the school there is little if any panic. And if the mother were to be allowed to stay in the classroom with the child there would generally be no fear. This is pathognomonic of the disorder. Accordingly, if the examiner has any question about the diagnosis this clinical test can most often resolve the problem.

Most often, the fear of school does not exist in isolation. Refusal is a common concomitant. Generally, the younger the child the greater is the fear element. And the older the child, the greater is the refusal element. But even the younger, panicky child will usually exhibit a refusal element. An adolescent is more likely to present as school refusal and may even rationalize the fear with professions of refusal. If the adolescent stays at home when not in school then the fear element is probably dominant. However, if the adolescent spends time with friends outside the home, then the disorder should more properly be referred to as a school refusal problem or truancy.

In the latter case, the term *school phobia*, or *separation anxiety*, is not appropriate in that the child is not exhibiting the characteristic dependent tie to the mother.

When leaving the home in the morning the child frequently complains of a variety of *physical symptoms:* headache, nausea, vomiting, diarrhea, fever, stomachache, low-grade fever, etc. (These somatic symptoms have led Schmitt (1971) to refer to the school phobic as "the great imposter.") These symptoms are usually physiological concomitants of the fear. Typically they are indulged by the mother, and it is difficult, if not impossible, to convince her that no physical disease is usually present. She may accuse the physician who advises her to ignore or not to indulge these symptoms of being insensitive and even deficient as a doctor for taking such a blasé attitude toward physical illness. She may also justify keeping the child home on the grounds that she doesn't wish to expose the other children in the classroom to possible communicable disease.

As mentioned, school phobic children usually rationalize their not going to school with explanations such as: the teacher is mean, they are bullied in the classroom, the school is boring, the work is too simple, the work is too hard. There may be a core of truth to many of these complaints. However, the other children are going to school in spite of these discomforts and indignities; the child with a separation anxiety disorder does not. Furthermore, attempts to reassure such children that things are not as terrible as they envision are of no avail. They remain adamantly unconvinced and will create new rationalizations if one is successful in dispelling previous ones. Often, as mentioned, the child genuinely does not know exactly what he or she is afraid of and will state so: "I don't know what I'm afraid of; I'm just scared." This may be an honest answer in that the child may not actually be aware of the underlying psychodynamic factors (to be discussed further) that are contributing to the anxiety.

Some children, if they can stay in the classroom, are still quite tense. They may have great difficulty concentrating on what the teacher is saying. This may be related to general anxiety, or they may be preoccupied with fears of harm befalling their mother. They may fantasize her becoming sick, or being injured, or may just have general fears that something terrible will happen to her while they are in school.

Waldfogel, Tessman, and Harbn (1959), in a two-year study, found that if the examiner goes into the school he or she will learn that there are many more cases of school phobia than would be suggested by the number of patients who come to a clinical office setting. The conclusion of their study was that only about one-third of school-phobic children come to the attention of mental health professionals.

ASSOCIATED FEATURES

It is rare in psychiatry to see an isolated phobia. In the 19th century especially, phobias were listed as separate disease entities, for example, claustrophobia (closed places), agoraphobia (open places), hypnophobia (sleep), and thanatophobia (death). These were artificial categorizations in that phobias rarely exist alone. And "school phobia" is no exception. Children with a separation anxiety disorder will often exhibit a wide variety of other fears. They may fear visiting other children's homes when unaccompanied by their mothers. Overnight visits may be impossible. Sleep-away camp is often unthinkable, and even summer day camps may be out of the question. These children are often afraid of the dark and will insist upon night-lights in their bedrooms. All children linger at bedtime and find a variety of excuses for keeping parents close by to help assuage the "separation anxiety" they experience before going to sleep. These children exhibit even more fears of such nighttime "separation."

Children with separation anxiety disorder may be afraid to go on errands in the neighborhood when other children their age are eager for such growth experiences. They may be afraid to stay in their rooms alone or venture alone into remote parts of their own homes, such as the attic or the basement. Many young children are afraid of dogs and other animals. These children persist in exhibiting such fears beyond the age when most children no longer manifest them. Many children, especially younger ones, are fearful when their parents go out for an evening. But these children are even more fearful of being left with babysitters and dread the prospect of their parents going out for an evening. They are usually more fearful of new situations than other children their age. And a whole list of other fears may be present, such as fear of monsters, muggers, strangers, plane travel, and dying.

In addition to the aforementioned fears, other personality difficulties are often present. These children tend to be demanding, coercive, and manipulative. This is especially the case with regard to the school situation. Upon being cajoled or pressured into going to school a child may state, "If you make me go to school, I'll jump out of the window." Unfortunately, the parents of these children tend to take such threats more seriously than is warranted. There is a grandiosity to these children that relates to the pampering and indulgence their parents provide. Often they act as if they were the masters and their parents the slaves. Coolidge *et al.* (1962) emphasize these children's exaggerated sense of infantile omnipotence. Leventhal and Sills (1964) proposed that a central personality characteristic of these children is their grandiose and unrealistic self-image. They too consider this to relate to the narcissism and feelings of omnipotence engendered by the parental overprotectiveness. They describe how these children's aggrandized self-image is threatened in the more egalitarian school situation, so they thereby crave to retreat home where their narcissistic gratifications can be indulged.

The traditional view is that the separation anxiety disorder is an entirely separate entity from the neurologically based learning disability. Although this is for the most part true, I believe there is a slight overlap. Specifically, I believe that if one were to compare children with separation anxiety disorder with, for example, children with obsessions or some other purely psychogenic symptom, one would find a higher percentage of neurologically based learning-disabled children in the separation anxiety group. I know of no studies on this issue, but I suspect that a factor in the anxiety of some of these children relates to their fear of exposure of their neurologically based learning disability. In short, the child avoids school to protect him- or herself from the exposure of the neurologically based learning problem. In the adolescent another kind of academic deficiency might contribute. Specifically, the adolescent may have been a poor student in lower grades and now is so far behind that school is a humiliating experience. An element in the fear then is that of exposure of the academic deficits.

PRECIPITATING FACTORS

Often, the precipitating factor is a situation that threatens the mother-child symbiotic tie. The mothers of these children are typically overprotective, and the central factor in the psychopathology is the pathological relationship between an overprotective mother and an overdependent child. Sometimes the threat to the relationship is realistic; sometimes it is only fantasized. Any situation that can potentially result in a disruption of the tie can be a precipitating factor. Commonly, a mother's illness may provide the threat—especially when hospitalization is required. The birth of a sibling may threaten the bond because of the extra attention that the newborn requires. The death of a significant figure may serve to precipitate a school phobia. The death of a grandparent, for example, may bring about the child's realization that we are all mortal—even mother. Sometimes the precipitating event can be the transfer to a new school or the moving of the family to a new neighborhood.

I remember well seeing two children whose school phobias were precipitated by the assasination of President John Kennedy. And in both cases it appeared as if the children were reasoning: "If the president of the United States—who is omniscient and omnipotent—can die, then no one is immune, even my mother."

It is important to appreciate that the precipitating event is not the sole factor in bringing about the symptomatology. It is best viewed as "the straw that broke the camel's back." One often obtains a history of milder fears of school attendance in earlier years. For example, because of inordinate fear of attending kindergarten, the mother may have waited a year and registered the child in the first grade. Traditionally, mothers are permitted to attend the first few days of nursery school and kindergarten. Then they are expected to leave. The mothers of these children may "hang in" longer and may even obtain the permission of the school authorities to do so. When other children reach the age when they are permitted to walk home alone, these children may continue to be accompanied by their mothers—even up to the high school period.

2

The Family Pattern

I present here the typical family pattern of the child with a separation anxiety disorder. It is important for the reader to appreciate that I am condensing here typical features from a variety of children with this disorder. One rarely sees a "pure" form. Each family will have its own special variations. However, the pattern I describe here is common enough to be considered typical.

THE MOTHER

I have referred frequently to the mother as the parent with whom the child has difficulty, not the father. This was not by pure chance or derived from some special personal reason for neglecting or omitting the father. The reality is that it is the mother-child tie, much more than the father-child tie, that is of significance in understanding the separation anxiety disorder. I will be devoting much more space to my description of the mother's role in the etiology of this problem than the father, although I will certainly have some things to say about the father.

More than anything else, these mothers are overprotective. They do not allow their children to ride bicycles on streets where

12

peers are being trusted to do so or to swim in deep water when other children their age are permitted. Running errands to distant neighborhoods is not allowed. Summer camp may be unthinkable. The mothers may consider parents who send their children off to such camps to be neglectful: "Parents who send their kids to summer camp just want to get rid of them. I would never do such a thing to *my* child." Day camps, however, may be permitted. Some of the children with separation anxiety disorder may not even be able to tolerate this degree of separation, but others can. I suspect that those children who do go are less threatened by the day camp situation because it is so filled with fun and games that they may be distracted from their phobic preoccupations.

These are the mothers who are forever peeking out the window to make sure that everything is all right in the street. They may not permit their children to play at such distance that they cannot easily be seen or heard. Even going around the corner may be too threatening. Some are given even less freedom because of dangers that are seen to exist in the neighborhood. Although there are certainly neighborhoods that are dangerous, other children are allowed to play, and the restrictions and warnings they are provided are far fewer than those given to the child with a separation anxiety disorder.

There may be a general atmosphere of secretiveness in the home which, in subtle ways, is a manifestation of the maternal overprotectiveness. The child may not be told about disturbing events that occur in the family, such as serious illness, divorce, or job loss. The child is viewed as not being able to handle such disturbing news and a conspiracy of silence may be entered into between the mother and other family members in order to protect the child.

The basic message that such mothers are giving to their children is this: "The world is a dangerous place and only I can protect you from the calamities that may befall you if you venture forth into it. If you always stay by my side, you will be protected from these dangers and all will be well with you. If you go forth without me, you may die!" This is the common element that lies beneath all of the aforementioned overprotective maneuvers. The child is repeatedly being told: "Watch out for this! Beware of that! Be careful of this! Stay away from that!" The child is being programmed with the message that there are dangers all around. The child is consistently being told that mother can be relied upon to protect him or her from these dangers. Thus, there is a fundamental conditioning element in the separation anxiety disorder. Focus on the underlying psychodynamics (to be discussed in detail in Chapter Three) often absorbs the attention and interest of the analytically-oriented therapist. Although focus on these underlying psychodynamics is important—even crucial—to successful treatment, one should not lose sight of this important conditioning factor in the separation anxiety disorder.

The mothers of these children are often phobic themselves. They may be agoraphobic in that they may be afraid to drive in open places, or even drive at all. They may be afraid of crowds or airplanes. They may be afraid to travel alone and thus tied down to their homes. Some are claustrophobics. Such mothers serve as models for their children's phobias. It is by identification with the parental model that we see another contributing factor. Eisenberg (1958) emphasized the mother's communication of her anxiety to the child. It is not so much by word as through gestures, attitudes, and facial expressions. The mother fears the cold, impersonal attitude of the school, and she serves as a model for such fear for her child. In addition, the mother's very life style reiterates the basic message that the world is a dangerous place. The mother sees dangers where others do not, or she exaggerates dangers that others consider to be mild.

In general, child psychiatrists do not give proper attention to the grandparental influence in the development of psychopathology. This is unfortunate because valuable information is lost by such inattention. Most psychogenic pathology is generations in the making. It can best be viewed as being handed down from one generation to the next. Although modifications certainly take place, the transmitted themes are often more similar than different as they go from one generation to the next. The child therapist should interview grandparents when possible. If this is not possible or practical, then a detailed description of the role (or absence of it) of the grandparent in the child's life should be assessed.

In the typical case of separation anxiety disorder the grandparental role is formidable. The key figure generally is the maternal grandmother.Typically, the mother is significantly dependent herself on the maternal grandmother. Although the mother may be in her 30s or 40s at the time of referral, there may not have been a day in her life when she did not either see or have telephone contact with the maternal grandmother. Rarely does the mother view this as a problem. Rather, she generally considers it to be a manifestation of the excellent relationship she enjoys with the maternal grandmother. She may say, "My mother and I have a wonderful relationship. We confide in each other completely. In fact, my mother knows much more about me than my own husband. And I know much more about her than even my father. She's my best friend. I feel we're like close sisters."

Commonly, the maternal grandmother overprotected the mother during childhood so that one is observing now the mother's adult manifestation of the dependent tie which she still has with the maternal grandmother. We tend to parent our children in the same way that our parents parented us. All of us model ourselves on the pattern of our parents, and part of that modelling involves parenting qualities. Although alterations are possible, and even common, the basic foundation of our parenting attitudes is laid down in our childhood. The child with a separation anxiety disorder, then, is best viewed as the third generation (at least) in a family in which overprotection of children (regardless of age) is an essential theme.

Grandparents can also play a more specific role in bringing about the disorder. Coolidge *et al.* (1962) described one case in which the impending death of the maternal grandmother intensified the mother's dependency needs, and this played a role in precipitating the child's illness. I personally have seen a number of cases in which the maternal grandmother actively indulged the child when at home. Sometimes the mother worked and the maternal grandmother was available to pamper the child when home from school. It may be extremely difficult to interrupt the overprotective pattern in such cases because of the ongoing availability of a grandparent in the home.

THE FATHER

The father of these children is typically passive. He generally views the mother as a "super-mother" and is unaware of the depth of the pathological relationship between the mother and the school-phobic child. He generally supports the mother's rationalization that other mothers are neglectful. He generally subscribes to the traditional view that the mother should be in complete control of child rearing and that fathers are the breadwinners. There is usually little conflict between the parents with regard to child rearing in that the father submits to the mother's "authority" in this area. He may rationalize such submission by subscribing to the "united front" theory which states that it is very bad for a child to observe parents disagreeing. By complying with this dictum he justifies submitting to the mother's will. But often there is little disagreement or submission because he passively accepts the mother's views regarding what is best for the child.

Such a father is often so dependent on the mother that he can be viewed as just another child in the household. He may be phobic himself and thereby serve as a model for the development of phobic reactions in the child. He may reiterate the mother's warnings about the dangers in the world. He does this with less conviction than the mother but parrots her warnings as a manifestation of his desire to please her.

Skynner and Robin (1976) described the typical father as passive in his relationship with his wife, often involving himself in a dependent-child relationship with the mother. They described the marital relationship as generally weak with the primary emphasis being on the parent-child bond. The family pattern is characteristically one in which there are strong vertical bonds running from parent to child, rather than between spouses.

3

Underlying
Psychodynamics

As is true of all forms of psychogenic pathology, the psychodynamic factors are multiple and complex. I present here those that I consider to be the most important. Again, they relate to the typical cases I have seen. It is extremely important for the examiner to explore these with an open mind and not enter the inquiry with the preconceived notion that any one of the factors I describe here is necessarily operative. The likelihood is that some of them will be; but the likelihood also is that others will not be present in a particular family under consideration.

THE CONDITIONED COMPONENT

As mentioned, these children have often been programmed for many years with the notion that the world is a dangerous place and that mother is the only one who can protect them from the catastrophes that await to befall them if they are to remove themselves from her protection. An important reason why such children fear going to school is that, for the first time, there is an enforced separation from the mother. Although the school doors are not actually locked, there is formidable social pressure for the child to remain there. The child who wants to go home is viewed as infantile, still "a baby," and is likely to suffer social stigma. In the school situation such children are captive. They are exposed to the dangers they have been taught await them when not under mother's protection. And they cannot readily run home to reassure themselves that their mothers are not suffering some calamity if this is one of their concerns.

This aspect of the psychodynamic factors contributing to the development of the child's school problems is justifiably referred to as a conditioned component of the school fear. It is just one manifestation of the generalized fears that the child has been conditioned to experience. The desensitization aspect of the therapeutic program addresses itself to this contribution to the child's symptomatology. Analytically-oriented and behavior therapists often view themselves as being proponents of contradictory theoretical persuasions and they provide therapeutic approaches that are exclusively consistent with their theories. I do not believe that such conflict is invariably necessary. Treatment of these children is a prime example. Some desensitization is warranted, not only for the conditioned fears that these children exhibit, but even for the phobic and anxiety factors in which there are complex psychodynamic contributions. A desensitization experience may still be helpful even when psychodynamic factors are operative. But, when the conditioned factor is contributing (as it most often is in these children), there is even a stronger argument for desensitization experiences in the therapeutic program. In Chapter Four I will discuss this aspect of the treatment in greater detail.

THE COMPLEMENTARY PSYCHODYNAMIC PATTERNS OF THE MOTHER AND CHILD

At this point I present what I consider to be a central psychodynamic pattern in the etiology of the separation anxiety disorder. To the best of my knowledge, this formulation has not been presented elsewhere. It comes from my observations of these children and their parents over many years. As is true for all psychodynamic formulations, it is a speculation. However, it is a speculation that I believe warrants serious consideration when one attempts to understand what is going on with these children and their families. To understand better this somewhat complex formulation, it is best to begin with the mother. As mentioned, she is often a dependent person, still dependent on the maternal grandmother. Consciously or unconsciously, she did not wish to leave the home of the maternal grandmother, but submitted to social pressures to leave the home and marry. However, she did so with a neurotic compromise in that she still maintained her dependent tie to the maternal grandmother. She may live close to the maternal grandmother or, if not, she still maintains very strong and frequent ties. Not only did she basically not wish to marry, but, in addition, she did not wish to assume the role of child rearer. Basically, she wished to remain a child in the home of her own mother. Accordingly, she resents the burden of raising her child and is basically angry at it. (Coolidge *et al.* [1962] emphasized this factor in the etiology of this disorder.) She cannot allow herself to accept these unloving feelings because of the guilt they would evoke in her. She deals with her hostility toward the child by reaction formation. Each time she envisions some calamity befalling the child she gratifies in fantasy her basic wish that the child die. But she is too guilty to accept the fact that she harbors such death wishes in her and so transforms the wish into a fear (an extremely common mechanism). It is not, then, that she *wishes* the child to be harmed, but that she *fears* that the child would be harmed. To fear a child's death is socially acceptable; to wish it is not. But the fantasy provides partial gratification of the wish, whether or not she views it as a wish or a fear. She tries to keep the child constantly at her side in order to reassure herself that her hostile wishes have not been fulfilled. Accordingly, she is forever peeking out the window to make sure that the child is fine and fears his or her going around the corner because from that vantage point she cannot reassure herself that the child has not been harmed. It is around the corner especially that the child may be hit by a car, mugged, raped, etc. In school, as well, she is deprived of such reassurance.

It is important for the reader to appreciate that when I say that these mothers harbor death wishes toward the child, I am not saying that they actually wish the child to be dead. Our unconscious minds utilize primitive mechanisms to represent thoughts and feelings, mechanisms that often "exaggerate to make a point." The child's being visualized as dead is a way of representing the hostility they harbor toward the child. It must also be appreciated that the mother's "death wishes" are really only part of her feelings toward the child. Like all human relations, the mother-child relationship is ambivalent. Deep loving feelings are present as well, and the mother of a school-phobic child would generally be devastated if her child were to die—the intense hostility notwithstanding.

The anger they originally felt at the prospect of rearing a child becomes intensified over the years as the demands on these mothers increase. She becomes increasingly angry at the child because of the drainage of her energy, and increasingly guilty over the direct expression of such resentment. Accordingly, there is a build-up of the reaction formation mechanism that serves, as mentioned, to allow for a fantasized expression of basic hostility without feeling guilty.

Interestingly, an almost identical pattern of psychopathology develops in the child. The child is basically angry at the mother for a number of reasons. Being kept from activities that other children enjoy produces social stigmatization. Other mothers are allowing their children to venture forth into areas in the community where these children are prohibited from entering. Being made more infantile is a source of anger. The children's excessive dependency on the mother is a source of frustration and irritation. The basic impairments in the mother's capacity to be a parent (more of which will be discussed later) are a source of deprivation for them. So deprived, these children become angry. They are not getting the same degree of healthy attention and affection as are children being reared in more stable homes. However, they cannot directly express this anger. They are much too fearful of doing that. They are much too dependent on their mothers to allow such expression. After all it is she, more than anyone else in the world, who has designated herself to be their protector from the dangers that await to befall them "out there." If resentment were to be expressed openly toward her they might lose her and then be exposed to the malevolent forces that ever await to pounce on unprotected children. So they must repress and suppress their hostility. And the children too come to deal with their hostility in the same way that their mothers do. Specifically, they use repression, reaction formation, and fantasized gratification. Each time they envision calamity befalling the mother, they satisfy in fantasy their own hostile wishes toward her. By turning the wish into a fear they assuage their guilt. They must be ever at their mother's side in order to reassure themselves that their hostile wishes have not been fulfilled. In this way, mother and child develop very similar psychodynamic patterns.

In this situation other difficulties develop which contribute to the entrenchment of the pathological tie. The parasite and the host basically come to hate one another. The host comes to hate the parasite because its blood is being sucked. And the parasite grows to hate the host because it is ever dependent on the host and, at the whim of the host, may be "flicked off" and then may die. Although the host gains the gratification of benevolence, altruism, and other ego-enhancing feelings, the basic resentment may counterbalance these benefits. Although the parasite may gain the gratifications of a "free meal," there is a precariousness to the situation that compromises this gratification. Being at the mercy of another person is not only ego debasing but frightening. And the frustrations associated with being in such a situation may ultimately produce resentment. The mother-child relationship in the separation anxiety disorder is basically a host-parasite one. And the anger so engendered in each feeds back into the aforementioned psychodynamic pattern. It becomes an additional source of anger which cannot be allowed expression in conscious awareness. It contributes thereby to an entrenchment of the repression, fantasized wish gratification, and reaction formation.

In short then the mother and child exhibit complementary psychopathology. However, more than complementing one another, the psychopathology is almost identical. It is almost as if the child's psychopathology is a rubber stamp of the mother's. Accordingly, a therapeutic approach that focuses on the child primarily, if not exclusively, is not likely to be successful. The forces in the mother that contribute to the maintenance of the pathological tie are great, and they are not likely to be altered significantly by a therapeutic program restricted to working with the child alone.

It is important for the reader to appreciate that what I describe as "new" in this formulation is the basic similarity between the psychodynamic patterns of the mother and child. The mechanisms of repression, fantasized gratification, and reaction formation are well-known mechanisms and have been described in a wide variety of psychogenic disorders. In addition, it is important to reiterate that when I say "death wish" here I do not believe that the mother really wants the child to die. In fact, were the child to die, it might very well be the greatest tragedy ever to befall the mother. Rather, I am referring to the primitive unconscious impulses that exist within all of us. All human relationships are ambivalent. All have a combination of hostile wishes and loving feelings. And the hostility, on occasion, can become formidable—to the point where there may be transient wishes that the other person be removed. When all is balanced out, the mother basically does not want the child dead. The death wish is a primitive expression of the intense hostile feelings that may exist in all relationships and which exists to a greater degree in both the mother and child when a separation anxiety disorder is present.

FURTHER FACTORS IN THE MOTHER'S OVERPROTECTIVENESS

There are other factors that are psychodynamically operative in the mother's overprotectiveness. The mother may be overprotective as a way of compensating for basic feelings of maternal inadequacy. By being a "super-mother" she can protect herself from the basic feelings of incompetence that she unconsciously feels. Her own mother was a poor model for mothering. Having low motivation for assuming the maternal role, she is not as likely to have acquired the techniques necessary for adequate parenting. Her need to denigrate the maternal capacity of other mothers is another way of bolstering her low sense of maternal adequacy. So we see here the compensation mechanism (another common defense mechanism) being utilized as well in the school phobia.

Another factor that contributes to the mother's overprotectiveness relates to vicarious gratification. As mentioned, the mother is basically dependent on the maternal grandmother. She has many unfulfilled dependency needs which she craves to satisfy. Those can be gratified by projecting herself psychologically into the position of her child. Each time she ministers to the child she is vicariously gratifying her own dependency needs. She is psychologically giving to her projected self. Each time she indulges and infantilizes the child she vicariously gratifies her own desire to be the recipient of such indulgence. This is also a common mechanism. It is at the root of compulsive benevolence. Many saint-like individuals are not as altruistic as they may appear. Although society may certainly derive great benefits from their benevolence, there are often contributing factors which are less than holy. This is one of them. Coolidge *et al.* (1962) described a related phenomenon in these mothers. Specifically, they fear that they will never be able to give enough to their children and are excessively guilty over minor child-rearing lapses. The authors believe that the mother's view that she can never give enough to her children relates to her identification with the child and her own dependency needs. Psychologically, she has projected herself out onto the child and her belief that the child never has enough is based on her basic belief that she can never have enough. In short, she projects onto the child her own dependency cravings.

DISPLACEMENT AND PROJECTION OF ANGER

Coolidge *et al.* (1962) described other factors that contribute to the repression and projection of anger. They postulate that the hostile fantasies of the child are projected onto the world and make the school a particularly dangerous place. Such hostility, however, is projected indiscriminately and other areas are considered dangerous as well. They also considered the mothers of these children to be inordinately uncomfortable with the child's anger. They harbor residua of their own childhood views that anger can destroy. Their overprotection serves to eliminate all overt expression of the child's anger. She may view the expression of anger to be devastating and may not be able to conceive of love and anger as coexisting. They may be significantly impaired in providing disciplinary and punitive measures because of their fear of the child's angry response. These attitudes contribute to the child's suppression and repression of hostility. Projection and displacement of hostility is commonly described in articles on school phobia. Prugh (1983) states: "The child's fear of separation is displaced onto the school, which he perceives as a dangerous place, and he projects his resentment about his parent's overcontrol and his fear of retaliation for that resentment, in the form of punishment, harm, or attack onto the school." This is a complex statement and is based on many speculations. Displacement of the fear of separation from the parents onto the school does not seem to me to be a reasonable explanation. Anger over the parent's overcontrol is certainly present, as is fear of retaliation for that resentment. To project the anger outward and to view the teachers as being angry at the child is also possible. The child then acts as if he or she were following the dictum: "It is not I that am angry, but it is the people at school." To then view the school as a punitive agent that will punish the child for his or her anger is a further mechanism that Prugh refers to that is somewhat speculative. The examiner does well to be cautious regarding a complete acceptance of the varied psychodynamic formulations that have been presented regarding the displacement factors in school phobia. The aforementioned reaction formation mechanism, in both mother and child, are in this examiner's experience the more common and reasonable.

OTHER PSYCHODYNAMIC FACTORS

Sexual inhibition problems in the parents may contribute. These "supermothers" may be so invested in their children that they have little investment in other activities, such as sex. And their passive-dependent husbands may relate to their wives in a mother-son pattern in which sex has little place. The mothers may be threatened by a sexual relationship with an adult male, but may be more comfortable with the milder sexuality of the mother-son relationship. In such situations the male child is used as a sexual-sensual surrogate by the mother. The processes by which this arrangement takes place are usually unconscious. It thereby warrants being a psychodynamic factor.

Another factor contributing to a child's separation anxiety disorder is the basic weakness of the parents. People who manifest phobic symptomatology are generally viewed as weak, both by themselves and by observers. One does not generally have confidence in an individual who is fearful. Having two parents who are both fearful is likely to contribute to feelings of insecurity in the child as he or she cannot rely upon either parent for strength and guidance in dangerous situations. The parents' primary way of dealing with danger (both real and fantasized) is by avoidance and flight. The dependency of the mother on the maternal grandmother deprives her of the reputation of being a strong, independent parent— something the healthy child very much needs. In addition, the passive-dependency of the father on the mother also deprives him of the reputation of being a strong parent. Even the maternal grandmother, who may be viewed as the matriarch, is basically a weak, frightened person who is forever predicting danger in the world and fleeing from or avoiding it.

Another psychodynamic factor relates to the pampering the child receives at home. The child is often viewed by the mother as "God's gift to the world." And the child tends to view himself or herself similarly. In school, however, no such idolization for the child is evident, and therefore the school situation may be intolerable. The mother, as well, may want to keep the child away from an environment in which he or she is not viewed with the adoration she considers to be proper for such a special person. In school her special child is just one of the crowd. As benevolent as the teacher may be, she is not going to indulge and pamper the child anywhere near the degree to that which occurs at home. The teacher may then come to be viewed as mean and rejecting by both the child and the mother. And this, of course, is considered to be another reason why the child should not go to school.

SPECIAL PSYCHODYNAMIC FACTORS OPERATIVE IN THE ADOLESCENT

In the adolescent youngster additional mechanisms may be operative. As mentioned, the refusal element may be more apparent than the phobic. If the youngster stays home, then it is likely that dependency on an overprotective mother is a central theme. If, however, the youngster does not go home when out of school, but rather stays with peers, it is likely that the problem does not warrant the term separation anxiety disorder. Furthermore, the adolescent is generally more embarrassed to exhibit fearful symptoms than the younger child. In fact, I have often been surprised about how little shame many young school-phobic children have over their symptoms. In their states of panic they may exhibit blood-curdling shrieks that cause teachers to run out of their classrooms wondering who is being murdered. And yet, most often they are not ashamed of these displays. The adolescent is much more likely to cover up fearful feelings and utilize refusal as the ostensible reason for not going to school.

Another factor in the adolescent separation anxiety disorder relates to the adolescent's appreciation that adult independence is close. The younger child tends to view adulthood as millions of years away. It is so remote that for all practical purposes it can be ignored. Adolescents cannot utilize such denial mechanisms. They have the bodies of adults and are capable of procreation. They may be physically taller and stronger than both parents. Such a situation may be very frightening, especially if they are ill equipped to deal with life at an age-appropriate level—as is often the case with school-phobic youngsters. In response adolescents may regress and entrench the dependent tie with the mother to provide protection from venturing forth into a demanding and less benevolent world. However, one rarely sees a separation anxiety disorder beginning in adolescence. Even when the overt symptomatology does manifest itself in adolescence, there have generally been many factors (such as those described above) that have contributed over the years. Some precipitating symptom may have brought the whole complex to a head, but there is generally a wealth of contributing factors that have antedated the appearance of the phobic symptoms.

CONCLUDING COMMENTS

I have described above what I consider to be the primary psychodynamic factors in the separation anxiety disorder. As mentioned, the therapist does well to appreciate that many of these may not be operative in a particular family being evaluated and treated. It is likely, however, that at least some of them will be. Each family must be considered distinct and unique and entitled to its own constellation of psychodynamic factors. To begin with the assumption that any particular pattern is automatically applicable may not only result in inadequate diagnosis, but will compromise significantly any treatment program based on such misapprehensions. I cannot emphasize this point too strongly. This phenomenon is often referred to as the utilization of "applied psychodynamics." The caveat is an important one, especially for the novice therapist, who often tends to compensate for lack of knowledge by applying onto the patient any psychodynamic formulation that appears reasonable.

4

General Therapeutic Considerations

CENTRAL ELEMENTS IN THE PSYCHOTHERAPEUTIC PROCESS

I view symptoms to represent maladaptive and inappropriate ways of dealing with the problems of life with which we are all confronted. The patient's selections of solutions to these problems have originally been devised because they appear to be the most judicious. What we refer to as psychodynamics are basically the pathways and processes by which these problems produce symptoms. Unfortunately, these inappropriate adaptations result in more trouble for the patient than less. Therapy involves helping people learn better ways of dealing with these inevitable conflicts and problems. Therapy must open up new options—options that may not have been considered by the patient previously, options that may not have been part of his or her repertoire. The utilization of these more adaptive solutions over time lessens the likelihood that the patient will have to resort to the maladaptive, symptomatic solutions.

In the context of a relationship between the therapist and the patient, it is highly desirable that each of the participants possess certain qualities if there is to be any likelihood of patients experiencing alleviation of the presenting symptomatology. The patient should be reasonably respectful of the therapist because of actual qualities that the therapist has that engender such respect. Idealization and idolizing of the therapist is antitherapeutic in that it creates unfavorable comparisons with the therapist that are ego-debasing to the patient and it makes it unlikely that the patient will relate realistically to other human beings who will inevitably reveal their deficits. The patient should be receptive to the therapist's comments, but not to the point of gullibility. There should be a reasonable desire to emulate qualities in the therapist that would serve the person well in life. As a result of such emulation, there will be some identification with the therapist's traits and values. (I do not believe that there is any psychotherapeutic interchange that does not involve some attempt on the therapist's part to transmit his or her values to the patient.) It is hoped that the values and qualities so taken on will be in the patient's best interests.

The therapist should have a genuine desire to help the patient. There should be a reasonable degree of sympathy (an intellectual process) and empathy (an emotional resonance) with the patient. There should be a reasonable capacity to identify with the patient, that is, put him- or herself in the patient's position. The therapist's goal should be that of *trying* to help the patient, but he or she should not feel that the failure to do so represents a failure in him- or herself.

In the context of such a relationship the therapist helps the patient learn better how to deal with the fundamental problems and conflicts of life with which we all are confronted and must deal in the course of our existence. The younger the patient, the more guidance, advice, and instruction the therapist should be willing to provide, and the older the patient, the more the therapist should facilitate the patient's finding his or her own solutions to these problems. However, even with the most mature adults, some guidance and instruction is warranted *after* the patient has made every reasonable attempt to resolve the problem him- or herself. Accordingly, the therapeutic process is very similar to the educational.

The therapeutic learning process occurs at many levels. I believe that the *least* efficacious is the intellectual. An intellectual insight acquired by the patient is, however, more useful than one provided by the therapist. When emotions are associated with intellectual learning, there is a greater likelihood of change. Metaphorical communications can be especially useful in this regard. This is not only true of children who traditionally enjoy stories, but adults as well in that they too will often learn better from a well selected anecdote or the relating of an experience by the therapist. Conceptualizations and abstractions are far less potent vehicles for clarifying issues than specific concrete examples, especially examples that relate to the patient's immediate experiences. And the most potent mechanism for modifying behavior is the experience. The old proverb, "A picture is worth a thousand words," is well-known. I would add to this, however, that "An experience is worth a million pictures." To the degree that the therapist can provide experiences, to that degree will he or she be able to bring about clinical change.

THE GENERAL STRUCTURE OF THE THERAPEUTIC PROGRAM

Waldfogel, Tessman, and Harhn (1959) emphasized the importance of early intervention as it relates to prognosis. The longer most diseases remain untreated, the poorer the prognosis. This is especially the case for the school phobia. The longer one allows the symptoms to be entrenched, the more difficult it becomes to get the child back to school. Children with separation anxiety disorder require an intensive therapeutic program. Optimally, they should be seen two to three times a week. Intensive work with the family—especially the mother—is crucial. As mentioned, without her active involvement the likelihood of successful treatment is very low. Ideally, the mother should be in treatment as well; however, she often has little insight into the fact that she has psychiatric problems and therefore has little motivation for meaningful therapy. In such cases she should be engaged on a counseling level. But even here, the therapist may meet with resistances—both conscious and unconscious. Although the father's participation in the treatment program is also advisable, my experience has been that he is most often unavailable. But even when he is available, his passivity and dependence on the mother make him an unlikely candidate for meaningful input into a therapy designed to bring about family change.

At the outset I attempt to lay down some very firm rules. The sessions are scheduled *after school*. I advise the parents that attempts must be made to get the child to school on time every morning. If, for whatever reason, the child does not make it in the morning, he must return to school after the lunch break. *After school* we can discuss what happened during the day and the reasons why the child is having difficulty. The parents are also instructed not to indulge the child at home if panic becomes so great that he has to return. Commonly, these children are allowed to watch television, play games, or otherwise enjoy their home activities. This only entrenches the problem. The parents are advised to create an atmosphere of "solitary confinement" as long as the child is home during school hours. They are urged to accept no excuse for not going to school. They should be discouraged from taking seriously minor complaints about physical illness and accepting as valid symptomatic complaints such as headache, dizziness, nausea, and stomachache. Only the most overt and definitely observable manifestations of physical illness should be accepted as a reason for the child's not going to school. And even then, it is preferable that the decision be made by the pediatrician or family doctor, rather than the mother or father.

The parents should be advised to push the child to the point of mild panic when urging him to go to school. They have to be helped to desensitize themselves to the blood-curdling screams and suicidal threats that these children may utilize in order to avoid the school situation. They have to be helped to appreciate that the fear element is only part of such antics and that the coercive element is usually very much there. The therapist must impress upon the parents that there should be no day on which there are not at least two attempts made (morning and lunch time) to get the child to school.

All this is part of the desensitization program and necessary to initiate at the outset. As mentioned, an important contributing factor in the development of the separation anxiety disorder is the conditioning process. The child has been programmed to view the world as a frightening place. Accordingly, a program of systematic desensitization is warranted as a direct therapeutic approach to this aspect of the problem. I do not, however, believe that there should be rewards given to the child. The reward for staying in school should be the ego enhancement that comes from having overcome the fear and the knowledge that one gains from the educational process. The reader may consider this a somewhat idealistic goal, especially for children who are school phobics. However, I believe that providing material rewards for academic performances is dangerous business. It directs the child away from the primary purpose of education— which is to learn for the gratification that knowledge provides.

In school, as well, the desensitization component of the therapeutic program should be utilized. This requires the dedicated cooperation of the school. The program that I prefer is one in which there is a progressive diminution in the time that the mother is allowed to remain in school. In addition, I do not suggest that attempts be made to get the child to go into his regular classroom from the outset. Rather, I suggest that he first be brought to a resource room or other place where he can join a small group of children being tutored. Ideally, there should be two or three students in such a group.

In addition, if possible, it is preferable that one of the students be a classmate, someone who is in the child's homeroom class and requires resource room supplementation. It is generally easier for a child to remain in school as part of such a small group than to enter into a classroom which may contain large numbers of children. The child receives more attention in the resource room and is more likely to develop a relationship with the teacher as a substitute for that which he or she has with the mother. Of course, there are many differences—especially the fact that the teacher is not likely to be anywhere near as indulgent as the child's mother.

Over time, the child should be encouraged to remain in the resource room for increasingly longer periods. Finally, attempts are made to have the child return for short periods to the regular classroom. Here, his accompanying the classmate from the resource room to his homeroom can be useful. The classmate then becomes a transitional person, somewhat similar to the resource room teacher. The classmate is a familiar figure who lends him- or herself well to being such a transitional person. This child makes it easier for the school-phobic child to return to the classroom. Again, progressively longer periods of toleration of the regular classroom routine are then encouraged.

Unfortunately, the cooperation that one gets from the parents of these children often leaves much to be desired. It is amazing how creative the mothers of these children can be with regard to the rationalizations and other excuses they can provide for not bringing the child to school and sabotaging the program. Every session they may come in with another excuse for not having followed the aforementioned recommendations. They may misinterpret, forget, and distort the instruction to the point where the total program may be subverted. The number of rationalizations is endless: "He had the sniffles yesterday and I didn't want to send him to school with a cold," "I felt his head and I'm sure that he had a temperature," "He looked pale and I was sure that he was coming down with something," "He told me that he was ready to vomit," "He stayed up late the night before and he just couldn't get up," "I didn't have the heart to push him, he looked so sad," "He threatened to kill himself if I sent him to school," "I forgot to set my alarm clock, so we got up too late. I didn't want to bring him to the classroom so late because he'd be embarrassed," "It was raining very heavily and I didn't want him to catch a cold," "I believe strongly that a child has to go three days without fever before I'll send him back to school," "I was sure that he was coming down with some infection and I didn't want the other children to catch anything," and so on.

Attempts to help such mothers appreciate that they are rationalizing and that they basically are contributing to the perpetuation of the child's illness often prove futile. I often try to impress upon such mothers the fact that nothing terrible will happen even if the child does come down with an illness while at school. Such advice is often responded to incredulously, with the mother wondering whether I am indeed a competent physician if I can make such a statement. I try to impress upon these mothers that we are not dealing with a patient who has had three heart attacks or two strokes and that illness in a setting where there is no immediate medical care will not prove fatal. Attempts to impress upon them the fact that the worst that can happen if the child becomes ill in school is that he will be returned home, is not generally responded to with receptivity. Rather, I am viewed as being insensitive, uncaring, and even defective when it comes to practicing good medicine. However, because I am "only a psychiatrist" my naiveté in this area is generally tolerated. In some cases, one can enlist the aid of the father. However, most often he too is swept up in the mother's delusion that she is a "super-mother" and that my advice would only be followed by the most negligent of parents.

As mentioned, the aid of the school is important. The school's cooperation varies. Some schools quickly provide home tutoring for the school-phobic child. This, in my opinion, is an academic "cop-out." It gets the school "off the hook." They need not involve themselves in the kind of desensitization program that is such an important part of these children's treatment. By allowing the child to remain at home they merely intensify the problem in that the child's mother is now being given educational and legal sanction to keep the child at home. There is probably no better way to entrench the pathological tie between the mother and the child. Providing the child with home tutoring enables the school to avoid the hassles involved in helping the child desensitize him- or herself to the phobic situation. A not inconsequential effect of home tutoring is that the child's education suffers inordinately. It is rare that such tutoring is provided for more than one to one-and-a-half hours a day. It is rare that it is more than a fraction of the educational exposure the child receives in school. Accordingly, the child falls even further behind and the home tutoring thereby increases the likelihood that he will be fearful of returning in the future. Sometimes the school needs a doctor's recommendation that the home tutoring is necessary for medical reasons. I have never signed such a recommendation, and cannot imagine myself ever signing one. It merely provides medical support for the school's copout. It is a medical contribution to the perpetuation of the problem. Hippocrate's caveat *Primum non nocere* is certainly applicable here. "Above all," he said, "do not harm." Basically, his view was that if you can't make the person better, at least you should not make him worse than he was before he came. Supporting a program of home tutoring contributes to the worsening of the pathology. We may not be able to help these children, but we should not be party to a program that makes them worse.

The school should be asked to tolerate to a reasonable degree these children's antics and disruptions. They may consider the aforementioned program to be inhumane and may view the therapist who recommends it to be at best insensitive and at worst sadistic. There is no question that pressuring these children into going to school may be viewed as cruel; however, it is no more cruel than giving an infant injections that may cause pain but may protect the child from a host of dreaded diseases. It is no more cruel than the surgeon who causes the child pain in the process of performing operative procedures that may be life saving. There are times when school authorities have appeared to agree with my recommendations, but have signified their acceptance of the program with comments such as "Well, you're the doctor" and "You must know what you're doing." Such "compliance" with the desensitization program may be disheartening, but it may be the best one can obtain from certain school personnel.

It is important for the reader to appreciate that the therapeutic approaches discussed thus far direct their attention to the symptomatic manifestations of the disorder. I view these as necessary parts of the treatment, but not central elements in the therapeutic approach. The therapist's primary attention should be directed to the underlying problems which are at the root of the disorder. These are the factors that have been elaborated upon in the aforementioned discussion of the psychodynamic factors that contribute to the development of the symptoms. With regard to the psychodynamic factors, there is the danger that the therapist will view the central underlying problems in a somewhat oversimplified fashion. To restrict oneself to the overprotection/overdependency problem is to take a narrow view of the child's difficulties. To focus on the phobia or the school is also to take a restricted view of the child's difficulties. These children are not simply afraid of school, summer camp, overnight visits, dogs, dark, strangers, deep water, running errands, snakes, and whatever else they may add to their list of feared objects. Rather, they are basically afraid of *life*. The *world* for them is indeed a dangerous place and they feel themselves helpless to cope with all the menacing forces that lie in wait for them. Our goal in therapy, then, is not simply to get the child back to school. The goal of therapy is to help these children reach an age-appropriate level of independence —especially with regard to functioning at an age-appropriate level regarding separation and independence from the mother.

It is this broader goal that one attempts to reach in the therapy of these children. The principle is well demonstrated by the case of Roberta, a 25-year-old woman, who came for treatment with the complaint that she had become progressively more fearful of leaving her home. The further the distance she went from her home the more panicky she became. Such a symptom is called agoraphobia. There are some who might utilize an approach involving desensitization. The program might include some kind of positive reinforcement for progressive toleration of separations from the home and some type of negative reinforcement when Roberta submitted to her fear of leaving her home.

An inquiry into her background revealed that her father died when she was 2 years old. She was an only child and her mother never remarried. The mother's main support was from social security, a pension the father received from his company, and insurance. This provided the mother with enough money to function at a lower-middle-class level and reduced the pressure on her to enhance her income by work outside the home. Further inquiry revealed that the mother did not begin the patient's schooling until the first grade, because "she cried the first day she went to kindergarten and I didn't want to cause her all that grief." Although the family home was only two blocks away from the school, the patient was brought to the school by her mother every day and met by her at the end of the school day. This situation prevailed right up to the junior-high-school level when the patient herself insisted that she could no longer tolerate the embarrassment of her mother's taking her to and from school each day. When the patient entered junior high school her mother warned her about the interests of boys. She described in detail the evils of sex and emphasized that boys should basically be distrusted because sex was the only thing they wanted from her. She was taught to distrust any other interest they might show and to view it as merely a cover-up for the primary desire to exploit her sexually. Inevitably, the boys made their advances and fulfilled thereby the mother's prophesy.

When Roberta entered high school, although a very good student, she was dissuaded from taking a college preparatory course. Her mother's main message to Roberta during the high-school period was that she hoped that she would never live to see the day when Roberta would leave her. Her plan was that Roberta would live at home after high school and obtain employment close by. However, during her final years in high school the warnings about men's sexual interests extended from classmates to all males—wherever the patient might encounter them.

Upon graduation from high school the patient applied only for jobs in the immediate vicinity of her home. Soon after beginning her first job in a clerical position, she brought home stories about the sexual interests of the men in her place of employment—confirming again her mother's predictions. When such interest was shown in the patient she became tense, withdrawn, and upset. Her mother encouraged her to leave her first job, but the same situation prevailed in her second and third. Within a year, with the encouragement of her mother, she stopped switching jobs and remained full time at home caring for her mother, who became increasingly dependent on her. During the next five years there was a gradual shift. Whereas in earlier years the patient was excessively dependent on her mother, in later years the mother became progressively dependent on Roberta. The mother's dependency became increasingly coercive and manipulative to the point where the patient became guilty when leaving the house (even for short periods) and extremely anxious. It was at 25 that she finally sought treatment for her fears of leaving the home.

In my opinion, a behavioral therapeutic approach, which would attempt to desensitize a patient such as Roberta, would not be likely to prove successful. It would focus too much on the external manifestations of the patient's difficulties. It loses sight of the broader problems with which such a patient suffers. To say that she suffers with agoraphobia only provides a translation into Greek of her presenting symptom. To say that she suffers from a fear of sexual encounters with men is also an oversimplification. In addition to sex, this young woman fears marriage, pregnancy, delivery, and child rearing. She fears an egalitarian relationship with a male. In fact, she fears an egalitarian relationship with any adult. She fears independence and self-assertion. She fears being an adult. In short, she is afraid of the world in general and retreats to the comfort of a symbiotic relationship with her mother. The aim of therapy, then, is not simply to help her desensitize herself to the anxieties associated with distancing herself from her mother. The aims of therapy are to help her grow up to become an independent, self-sufficient human being capable of functioning in the world as an adult—with all the complexities, demands, frustrations, and gratifications attendant to such growth.

Although Roberta is an adult, her case is presented because it demonstrates the aims of therapy of the child suffering with a separation anxiety disorder. The goal of treatment is not simply to get the child back to school. The goal of treatment is to help the youngster function at an age-appropriate level. The goal of treatment is to break the pathological tie with the mother to the extent that the youngster can function with a degree of independence appropriate for his age. This goal should be viewed as a stepping stone toward progressively greater emancipation as the child grows older. If the treatment is successful, the child will not end up like Roberta.

THE USE OF MEDICATION

It would appear that anxiolytic agents would be the drugs of choice in the separation anxiety disorder. I do use such drugs, but I am careful to point out to both the parent and the child that they can only serve a minor role. Believing as I do that underlying family problems are central to the development of the disorder, I do not wish to convey the notion that the whole difficulty can be dispelled by a drug. The drug that I have most frequently used is diazepam (Valium). I generally start with two to four milligrams in the morning and at lunch time. I then progressively increase the dose—often to the sublethargic level. Although anxiolytic agents may contribute somewhat to the reduction of the child's anxiety, one runs the risk that they will interfere, as well, with the learning process because of the lethargic side effects one sees with higher doses. I will generally tell these children that the medication will probably *help* them to be less scared, but that they cannot expect it to solve the whole problem. I emphasize that their own willpower will be required and that we will have to discuss *after school* some of the family problems that are contributing to their fears.

Gittelman-Klein (1975) and Gittelman-Klein and Klein (1973) are strong proponents of the use of the tricyclic antidepressant imipramine in the treatment of the separation anxiety disorder. Although they do not believe that most of these children are necessarily suffering with an underlying depression, they consider these agents to be capable of blocking the peripheral physical manifestations of the panic state. Gittelman-Klein and Klein point out, however, that psychotherapy is also warranted in the treatment of these children. Although my own experience with imipramine in the treatment of the separation anxiety disorder has been limited, I have not been significantly successful with its utilization. I have not found it to be as effective as diazepam in reducing the symptomatology. I cannot deny that a depressive factor is part of these children's symptom picture. But I do not believe it to be the foundation upon which the symptoms are built. I believe the depression one sees is secondary to all the grief these children suffer in association with their illness. I do not believe it to be the kind of endogenous depression that is more likely to respond to imipramine. Furthermore, I have not observed imipramine to have the blockage effect that Gittelman-Klein and Klein describe.

CONCLUDING COMMENTS

I have described in this chapter the general structure of the therapeutic program for children with separation anxiety disorder. In general, I have found myself more authoritarian when structuring therapeutic approaches to these children than I have with children who are suffering with other disorders. This is true for both the mother and the child. The mothers tend to be most creative in inventing excuses for overprotecting their children and not sending them to school. And the children's panicked states and coercive maneuvers make them particularly unreceptive to my strong insistence that they go to school. Because the fathers of these children are so often passive and dependent, one would think that they would be more receptive to the therapist's instructions. However, I have not found this to be the case. They find themselves in the middle of a conflict between their wives and the therapist and will generally support their wives' position because of their extreme dependency.

Although these might be considered discouraging drawbacks of the therapeutic program, my experience has been relatively good with regard to the successful treatment of these children. All therapeutic programs have their compromises and the treatment of children with separation anxiety disorder is no exception. It behooves therapists to know the drawbacks of the therapeutic programs they are utilizing, just as it behooves physicians to be aware of the untoward side effects of the drugs they are prescribing. These are problems to be worked through, circumvented, and avoided and should not be reasons for not attempting treatment.

In this chapter I have presented the broad outline of the general therapeutic program. In the next two chapters I will go into specific aspects of the treatment of these children and their families. In the next chapter I will describe in detail certain therapeutic techniques that I have found particularly useful in the treatment of these children. In the following chapter I will describe in detail the specific methods I have found useful in my work with these children and their parents.

5

Special
Therapeutic Techniques

The psychotherapeutic approaches I utilize in the treatment of children with psychogenic learning disabilities will be made more meaningful if the therapist is acquainted with some special therapeutic approaches I employ in these children's treatment. My purpose here is not to describe the wide variety of therapeutic techniques that I use, but to focus on three that I utilize extensively. Two (*The Mutual Storytelling Technique* and *The Talking, Feeling and Doing Game*) are instruments that I have devised myself. The third, *utilization of the parent as an "assistant therapist,"* is certainly not an original idea of mine, but there are some special ways in which I use the parent that warrant discussion.

THE MUTUAL
STORYTELLING TECHNIQUE

The use of children's stories as a source of psychodynamic information is well known to child psychotherapists. To the best of my knowledge, this was first described in the literature (in German) by

Hug-Hellmuth in 1913. (The first English Translation appeared in 1921.) A fundamental problem for the child therapist has been that of how to take the information that one can derive from such stories and bring about psychotherapeutic change. Children's stories are generally easier to analyze than the dreams, free associations, and other verbal productions of adults. Often, the child's fundamental problems are exhibited clearly to the therapist, without the obscurity, distortion, and misrepresentation characteristic of the adult's fantasies and dreams.

A wide variety of psychotherapeutic techniques have been devised to use therapeutically the insights that the therapist can gain from children's stories. Some are based on the assumption, borrowed from the adult classical psychoanalytic model, that bringing into conscious awareness that which has been unconscious can in itself be therapeutic. The literature is replete with articles in which symptomatic alleviation and even cure quickly follows the patient's gaining insight into the underlying psychodynamic patterns. My own experience has been that very few children are interested in gaining conscious awareness of their unconscious processes in the hope that they can use such insight to alleviate their symptoms and improve their life situation. I believe that one of the reasons for this is that the average child of average intelligence is not cognitively capable of taking an analytic stance and engaging in a meaningful psychoanalytic inquiry until about the age of 10. This corresponds to Piaget's level of formal operations, the age at which the child can consciously differentiate between a symbol and the entity which it symbolizes.

Of course, brighter children are capable of doing this at early ages. But even those children are generally not interested in assuming the analytic stance and delving into the unconscious roots of their problems—unless there are significant environmentally stimulating factors. The child who grows up in a home in which both parents are introspective and analytic is more likely to think along these lines as well. Accordingly, it is only on rare occasions that I do direct analytic work with children under the age of 10 or 11. And when this occurs, it is usually a patient who, 1) is extremely bright, and 2) comes from a home in which the parents have been or are in psychoanalytic treatment themselves, and who in addition, are deeply committed to introspective approaches to dealing with life's problems. But even in adult therapy, professions of commitment to analysis notwithstanding, most of my patients are not deeply committed to psychoanalytic inquiry. And they are generally even more resistant to analyzing their resistances to such inquiry. Hence, I attempt to employ a psychoanalytic approach to the therapeutic utilization of children's stories very infrequently.

In the 1920s Anna Freud and Melanie Klein—both influenced deeply by Hug-Hellmuth's observation—attempted to work analytically with children, and the analysis of their stories was essential to their therapeutic approaches. Although they differed significantly regarding the interpretations they gave to children's stories, they agreed that the gaining of insight into the story's underlying psychodynamic meaning was crucial to meaningful therapeutic change. Beginning in the 1930s Conn (1939, 1941a, 1941b, 1948, 1954) and Solomon (1938, 1940, 1951, 1955) described the same frustrations this examiner experienced with regard to getting children to analyze meaningfully their self-created stories. They were quite happy to analyze those children who were receptive to such inquiries. But for those who were not, they were equally satisfied discussing the child's story at the symbolic level. They believed that therapeutic changes could be brought about by communicating with the child at the symbolic level. For example, if a child told a story about a dog biting a cat and was unreceptive to analyzing it, they found that discussions about why the dog bit the cat and what better ways there were to handle the situation could get across important messages without producing the anxiety of analytic inquiry.

During my residency training in the late 1950s I first began to suffer the frustration of children's unreceptivity to analysis. I was much more comfortable with the work of Conn and Solomon. It was from these experiences that I derived in the early 1960s the technique that I subsequently called *The Mutual Storytelling Technique*. Basically, it is another way of utilizing therapeutically children's self-created stories. It stems from the observation that children enjoy not only telling stories but listening to them as well. The efficacy of the storytelling approach for imparting and transmitting important values is ancient. In fact, the transmission of such values was and still is crucial to the survival of a civilized society. Every culture has its own heritage of such stories that have been instrumental in transmitting down the generations these important messages.

The Basic Technique

In this method the therapist elicits a self-created story from the child. The therapist then surmises its psychodynamic meaning and then tells a responding story of his or her own. The therapist's story utilizes the same characters in a similar setting, but introduces healthier resolutions and adaptations of the conflicts present in the child's story. Because the therapist is speaking in the child's own language —the language of allegory—he or she has a better chance of "being heard" than if the messages were transmitted directly. The direct, confrontational mode of transmission is generally much more anxiety provoking than the symbolic. One could almost say that with this method the therapist's messages bypass the conscious and are received directly by the unconscious. The child is not burdened with psychoanalytic interpretations that are generally alien and incomprehensible to him. With this technique, one avoids direct, anxiety-provoking confrontations so reminiscent of the child's experiences with parents and teachers.

The technique is useful for children who will tell stories, but who have little interest in analyzing them (the vast majority, in my experience). It is not a therapy per se, but one technique in the therapist's armamentarium. Empirically, I have found the method to be most useful for children between the ages of 5 and 11. I generally do not treat children under the age of 4 (I find it more efficient to counsel their parents). In addition, children under the age of 5 are not generally capable of formulating organized stories. In the 4- to 5-year age bracket, one can elicit a series of story fragments from which one might surmise an underlying psychodynamic theme which can serve as a source of information for the therapist's responding story. The upper age level at which the technique is useful is approximately 11. At that time, children generally become appreciative of the fact that they are revealing themselves. They may rationalize noninvolvement with the technique with such justification as, "This is baby stuff," and "I don't feel like telling stories." Lastly, the technique is contraindicated for children who are psychotic and/or who fantasize excessively. One wants more reality oriented therapeutic approaches such as *The Talking, Feeling, and Doing Game* (to be discussed subsequently) or else one may entrench their pathology.

Dolls, drawings, and other toys are the modalities around which stories are traditionally elicited in child psychotherapy. Unfortunately, when these facilitating stimuli are used, the child's story may be channeled in highly specific directions. They have a specific form that serve as stimuli that are contaminating to the self-created story. Although the pressure of the unconscious to create a story that serves a specific psychological purpose for the child is greater than the power of the facilitating external stimulus to contaminate the story, there is still some contamination when one uses these common vehicles for story elicitation. The tape recorder does not have these disadvantages; with it, the visual field remains free from distracting and contaminating stimuli. The tape recorder almost asks to be spoken into it. Eliciting a story with it is like obtaining a dream on demand. Although there are differences between dreams and self-created stories, the story that is elicited by a tape recorder is far closer to the dream than that which is elicited by play material.

In earlier years I used an audio tape recorder. In more recent years I have used a video tape recorder. For the therapist who has this instrument available, it can enhance significantly the child's motivation to play the game. Although hearing one's story on the audio tape recorder can serve to facilitate the child's involvement in the game, watching oneself on television afterwards is a much greater motivating force. But the examiner should not conclude that these instruments are crucial. They are merely devices. Long before they were invented children enjoyed relating self-created stories, and the therapist should be able to elicit them from most children without these contrivances. They should be viewed as additional motivating facilitators and, of course, they have the additional benefit of the playback which provides reiteration of the therapeutic messages. In earlier years many children would bring their own tape recorder and simultaneously tape the stories with me, and then listen to them at home for further therapeutic exposure. Recently, I added a second video cassette recorder to my office closed-circuit television system. A child can now bring his or her own video cassette (to be found with increasing frequency in homes these days), tape the story sequences along with me, and then watch him- or herself at home.

Specific Techniques
for Eliciting Self-Created Stories

I begin by telling the child that we are now going to play a game in which he or she will be guest of honor on a make-believe television program. In earlier years I would ask the child if he or she would like to be the guest of honor on the program; in more recent years I seduce him or her into the game without the formal invitation. Of course, if the child strongly resists, I will not pressure or coerce. We then sit across the room from the mounted camera, and the video-cassette recorder, lights, and camera are turned on. I then begin:

Therapist: Good morning, boys and girls. I would like to welcome you once again to Dr. Gardner's "Make-Up-a-Story Television Program." We invite boys and girls to this progam to see how good they are at making up stories. The story must be completely made up from your own imagination. It's against the rules to tell stories about anything that really happened to you or anyone you know. It's against the rules to tell a story about things you've read about, or heard about, or seen in the movies or on television. Of course, the more adventure or excitement the story has, the more fun it will be to watch on television later.

Like all stories, your story should have a beginning, a middle, and an end. And after you've made up your story, you'll tell us the lesson or the moral of your story. We all know that every good story has a lesson or a moral. Then, after you've told your story, Dr. Gardner will make up a story also. He'll try to tell one that's interesting and unusual, and then we'll talk about the lesson or the moral of his story.

And now, without further delay, let me introduce to you a boy(girl) who is with us for the first time. Tell us your name young man(woman).

I then ask the child a series of questions that can be answered by single words or brief phrases. I will ask his or her age, grade, address, name of school, and teacher. These "easy" questions reduce the child's anxiety about the more unstructured themes involved in "making up a story." I then continue:

Therapist: Now that we've heard a few things about you, we're all interested in hearing the story you've made up for us today.

Most children at this point begin with their story, although some may ask for "time out to think." Of course this request is granted. There are some children, however, for whom this pause is not enough, but will still want to try. In such instances the child is told:

Therapist: Some children, especially when it's their first time on this program, have a little trouble thinking of a story. However, I know a way to help such children think of a story. Most people don't realize that there are *millions* of stories in everyone's head. Did you know that there are millions of stories in your head? (Child usually responds negatively.) Yes, right here between the top of your head and your chin (I touch the top of the child's head with one finger, and the bottom of his or her chin with another finger), right between your ears (I then touch the child's two ears), inside your brain which is in the center of your head are millions of stories. And I know a way how to get out one of them.

The way to do this is that we'll tell the story together. And this way, you won't have to do all the work yourself. The way it works is that I start the story and, when I point my finger at you, you say exactly what comes into your mind at the time that I point to you. You'll see then that your part of the story will start coming into your brain. Then after you've told the part of the story that comes into your mind, I'll tell another part, and then I'll point to you. Then we'll go back and forth until the story is over. Okay, here we go. (The reader will note that I again did not ask the child if he or she wished to proceed, rather I just "rolled on.")

Okay, here we go (I now speak *very slowly*). Once upon a time ... a long, long time ago ... in a distant land ... far, far away ... far beyond the mountains ... far beyond the deserts ... far beyond the oceans ... there lived a ...

I then quickly point my finger at the child. It is a rare child who does not offer some associative word at that point. For example, if the word is "cat," I will then say, "And *that* cat ..." and once again point firmly to the child, indicating that it is his or her turn to tell more of the story. I follow the next statement provided by the child with, "And then ..." or "The next thing that happened was...." Or, I will repeat the last few words of the patient's last sentence, with such intonations that continuation by him or her is implied. Every statement the child makes is followed by some connective term supplied by me and indicates to the child that he or she should supply the next statement. At no point do I introduce any specific material into the story. The introduction of such specific phrases or words would defeat the purpose of catalyzing the child's production of his or her *own* created material and of sustaining, as needed, its continuity.

This approach is successful in eliciting stories from the vast majority of children. However, if it is unsuccessful, it is best to drop the activity in a completely casual and nonreproachful manner, such as: "Well, today doesn't seem to be your good day for storytelling. Perhaps we'll try again some other time."

While the child is telling his or her story, I jot down notes. These help me analyze the story and serve as a basis of my own. When the child completes the story, I then elicit its lesson or moral. In addition, I may ask questions about specific items in the story. My purpose here is to obtain additional details which are often helpful in understanding the story. Typical questions might be: "Is the dog in your story a boy or a girl, a man or a woman?" "Why did the horse do that?" or, "Why was the cat so angry at the squirrel?" If the child hesitates to provide a lesson or a moral, or states that there is none, I will usually reply: "What, a story without a lesson? Every good story has *some* lesson or moral! Every good story has something we can learn from it."

Usually, after completing my story, I will ask the child to try to figure out the moral or the lesson of my story. This helps me ascertain whether my message has been truly understood by the child. If the child is unsuccessful in coming forth with an appropriate lesson or moral to my story, I will provide it. Following the completion of my story, I generally engage the child in a discussion of its meaning to the degree that he or she is capable of gaining insight and/or referring the story's message to him- or herself. Many children, however, have little interest in such insights, and I do not press for them. I feel no pressure to do so because I believe that the important therapeutic task is to get across a principle, and that if this principle is incorporated into the psychic structure (even unconsciously), then therapeutic change can be brought about.

Fundamentals of Story Analysis

Obviously, the therapist is in no position to create a story of his or her own unless there is some understanding of the basic meaning of the child's story. The greater the familiarity with the child, the greater the likelihood the therapist will be in the position to do this. Also, the more analytic training and experience a therapist has, the more likely he or she will be able to ascertain correctly the meaning of the child's story. I first try to ascertain which figure(s) in the child's story represent the child him- or herself and which symbolize significant individuals in the child's milieu. Two or more figures may represent various aspects of the *same* person's personality. There may, for example, be a "good dog" and a "bad dog" in the same story, which are best understood as conflicting forces within the same child. A horde of figures, all similar, may symbolize powerful elements in a single person. A hostile father, for example, may be symbolized by a stampede of bulls. Malevolent figures can represent the child's own repressed anger projected outward, or they may be a symbolic statement of the hostility of a significant figure. Sometimes both of these mechanisms operate simultaneously. A threatening tiger in one boy's story represented his hostile father, and the father was made more frightening by the child's own hostility, repressed and projected onto the tiger. This is one of the reasons why many children view their parents as being more malevolent than they actually are.

Besides clarifying the particular symbolic significance of each figure, it is also important for the therapist to get a general overall "feel" for the atmosphere of the story. Is the ambiance pleasant, neutral, or horrifying? Stories that take place in frozen wastelands or on isolated space stations suggest something very different from those that occur in the child's own home. The child's emotional reactions when telling the story are of great significance in understanding its meaning. An 11-year-old boy who tells me, in an emotionless tone, about the death fall of a mountain climber reveals not only his anger but also the repression of his feelings. The atypical must be separated from the stereotyped, age-appropriate elements in the story. The former may be very revealing, whereas the latter rarely are. Battles between cowboys and Indians rarely give meaningful data, but when the chief sacrifices his son to Indian gods in a prayer for victory over the white man, something has been learned about the boy's relationship with his father.

The story may lend itself to a number of different psychodynamic interpretations. It is part of the creativity of the unconscious, even in the child, that these can be fused together in the same symbols. The themes may exist simultaneously or in tandem. In selecting the theme that will be most pertinent for the child at that particular time, I am greatly assisted by the child's own lesson or moral. It will generally tell me which of the various themes is most important for the storyteller him- or herself. At times, however, the child may not be able to formulate a relevant moral or lesson. This is especially the case for younger children and/or older ones with cognitive or intellectual impairment. In such cases the therapist is deprived of a valuable source of information.

I then ask myself: "What is the main pathological manifestation in this story?" or, "What is the primary inappropriate or maladaptive resolution of the conflicts presented?" Having identified this, I then ask myself: "What would be a more mature or a healthier mode of adaptation than the one utilized by the child?" I then create a story of my own. My story generally involves the same characters, setting, and initial situation as the child's story. However, very quickly my story evolves in a different direction. The pathological modes are not utilized although they may be considered by various figures in the story. Invariably, a more appropriate or salutary resolution of the most important conflict(s) is achieved.

In my story I attempt to provide the child with more *alternatives*. The communication that the child not be enslaved by his or her psychopathological behavior patterns is crucial. As mentioned in the previous chapter, therapy, if it is to be successful, must open new avenues not previously considered by the patient. It must help the patient become aware of the multiplicity of options that are available to replace the narrow, self-defeating ones that have been selected. After I have completed my story, I attempt to get the patient to try to figure out its lessons or morals. It is preferable that the child do this, but if the child cannot, then I present it for them. (It is nowhere written that a story must have only one lesson or moral.) My lesson(s) attempts to emphasize further the healthier adaptations I have included in my story. If, while telling my story, the child exhibits deep interest or reveals marked anxiety, then I know that my story is "hitting home." I know then that I am on the right track, and that I have ascertained correctly the meaning of the story and have devised a responding story that is relevant. The anxiety may manifest itself by jitteriness or increased activity level. If the child is bored, it may mean that I am off point. However, it may also be a manifestation of anxiety, and the therapist may not know which explanation is most relevant.

Following the completion of my story and its moral, I usually try to engage the child in a discussion of our stories. For the rare child who is interested in gaining insight, we will try to analyze our stories. For the majority there may be a discussion along other lines, and these are usually at the symbolic level. In earlier years, when I used the audio tape recorder, children were sometimes interested in listening to the tape. In more recent years, since I have been utilizing the video cassette recorder, the interest in watching the program has been much greater. Playing the program makes possible a second exposure to the messages I wish to impart. And, as mentioned, I have recently purchased a second video cassette recorder—which enables the child to bring his or her own tape and replay it at home. This not only provides the opportunity for reiteration of the therapeutic messages, but also serves to entrench the therapist-patient relationship.

Concluding Comments

I have described the basic rationale of *The Mutual Storytelling Technique.* I do not claim to have invented a new method of treatment. The principle is an ancient one, and many therapists have no doubt utilized the method. I believe that my main contribution lies in having written articles on the subject and having formulated more specific criteria for analyzing and creating stories. The utilization of the method in the treatment of a wide variety of psychiatric disorders of childhood is discussed in a number of other publications of mine (Gardner 1968; 1969; 1970a,b; 1971a; 1972a,b; 1973a; 1974a,b,c; 1975a,b,c; 1976; 1979a,b; 1980; 1981; 1983a). A comprehensive description of the details of utilizing the technique (with regard to story analysis and the therapist's story creations) is given in a full-length text on the subject (Gardner, 1971b).

THE TALKING, FEELING, AND DOING GAME

The Mutual Storytelling Technique was devised in the early 1960s. Many children readily involved themselves in the game, and it was a central therapeutic modality throughout the course of their treatment. Others however were unreceptive. It was for these children that I devised a series of other games which basically increased the likelihood that the child would tell stories. This was accomplished by providing token reenforcement in the context of a variety of board-type games as well as the utilization of play material in a mildly competitive format. These games were developed in the late 1960s and are described in detail elsewhere (Gardner 1975,a,b). These proved useful in facilitating the child's telling self-created stories and providing other fantasy material that was of value in therapy. However, there were some children who, in spite of the attractiveness of these games, still could not or would not tell stories. It was for these children that I devised in the early 1970s *The Talking, Feeling, and Doing Game* (1973b; 1974d; 1975a,b,c,d; 1976; 1979b; 1983b).

The Basic Format
of The Talking, Feeling, and Doing Game

The game is similar in appearance to the typical board games with which most children are familiar (Figure 1). It includes a playing board, dice, playing pawns, a spinner, a path along which the pawns are moved, reward chips, and cards that are drawn from the center of the game board. This familiarity, as well as the fact that it is a *game,* reduces initial anxieties and attracts the child to the therapeutic instrument.

To begin the game both the therapist and the child place their colored pawns at the START position. Alternatively, they throw the dice and move their pawns along a curved path of squares which ultimately end at the FINISH position. For younger children, one die can be used. A pawn can land on one of a number of squares: white, red, yellow, SPIN, GO FORWARD (a specific number of squares), and GO BACKWARD (again, a specific number of squares). If the pawn lands on a white square, the player takes a Talking Card; on a yellow square, a Feeling Card; and on a red square, a Doing Card. If the pawn lands on SPIN, the player spins the spinner and follows the directions. Generally, these provide gain and loss of chips, or forward and backward movement of the playing pawn. Similarly, landing on GO FORWARD or GO BACKWARD squares results in movement of the pawn. The spinner and movement squares are of little, if any, psychological significance. They are included to ensure the child's fun and relieve some of the pressure associated with a

Figure 1

high frequency of drawing only the aforementioned three types of cards.

Of course the core of the game is the directions and questions on each of the cards. As their titles imply, the Talking Cards instruct the player to make comments that are primarily in the intellectual and cognitive area. The Feeling Cards focus primarily on affective issues. The Doing Cards usually involve play acting and/or some kind of physical activity. The child is given a reward chip for responding to each of the cards. Although a token reinforcement is provided, the game is by no means a form of behavior therapy. Positive reinforcement is not being given for behavioral change at the manifest level. Rather, the child is being reinforced for providing psychodynamically meaningful material for psychotherapeutic utilization. The child's and the therapist's responses are used as points of departure for psychotherapeutic interchange.

There is no actual time limit for the game. Both the therapist and the patient play similiarly, and each responds to the cards. The first player to reach the FINISH position receives five extra reward chips. The second player continues to play until he or she also reaches the FINISH position. If the game is interrupted prior to one player's reaching the FINISH position, the player who is closest to that position receives three extra reward chips. The therapist should discourage active competition on the child's part for the acquisition of chips. The game should be played at a slow pace, and each response should serve as a point of departure for psychotherapeutic interchange.

There are 104 cards in each stack. I always randomize them and have never "stacked the deck" with specific cards that I hope the child will draw. The cards are so designed that any card will be relevant to any player. About 5% of the cards in each stack are so simple and nonthreatening that just about any child will respond. These are basically placed there for the extremely fragile child who would be threatened by the cards that will touch on basic problems of living. These simpler cards ensure that the child will get chips and thereby remain motivated to participate in the game. The most liberal criteria are used when deciding whether or not a child should be given a chip for responding. Again, the therapist wants to do everything possible to draw the child in and maintain his or her interest. Some typical low-anxiety cards: "How old is your father?"; "What's your lucky number? Why?"; "What is your telephone number?";

"What is your address?"; "What's your favorite flavor ice cream?"; "What present would you like to get for your next birthday?"; "What's your favorite smell?" "Make believe you're blowing out the candles on your birthday cake."; and "Make a funny sound with your mouth. If you spit, you don't get a chip."

The remaining questions and directions are far richer psychologically and are at the "heart" of the game. These are not as anxiety provoking as a request to make up a story that will reveal free fantasies; however, they provide highly meaningful therapeutic material. Some typical cards: "All the girls in the class were invited to a birthday party except one. How did she feel? Why wasn't she invited?"; "Everybody in the class was laughing at a girl. What had happened?"; "A boy has something on his mind that he's afraid to tell his father. What is it that he's scared to talk about?"; "What's the worst thing a boy can say to his mother"; "Suppose two people were talking about you, and they didn't know you were listening. What do you think you would hear them saying?"; "What things come into your mind when you can't fall asleep?"; "If the walls of your house could talk, what would they say about your family?"; "Tell about something you did that made you proud."; and "What's the worst thing that ever happened to you in your whole life?".

The child's responses are usually revealing of the psychological issues that are most relevant to him or her at that point. The questions and instructions cover the wide range of human experiences. The material elicited is likely to be relevant to the etiology of the child's disturbance. The questions are designed to direct the child's attention to the basic life conflicts which are being resolved in inappropriate and maladaptive ways by the symptomology. They direct the child's attention to the issues that I referred to previously, that is, the basic life conflicts that are at the foundation of psychopathological processes. As mentioned, each response serves as a point of departure for therapeutic interchanges. The therapist does not merely provide the child with a chip and then race on with the game to see who can reach FINISH first. Rather, the therapist tries to get "as much mileage" as possible from each response, using his or her discretion in deciding how much discussion is warranted for each patient. Highly defensive and resistant children will not be able to tolerate the kind of in-depth discussion in which the healthier child can readily participate.

The therapist answers the same questions as the child. The

greater the therapist's knowledge of the child's problems, the more judicious will be his or her responses. Obviously, it is not the therapist's role to provide answers relevant to his or her *own* life problems. Rather the responses should be designed to provide therapeutic messages pertinent to the child's difficulties. I always respond honestly. Often I will provide a response that will relate to an experience of mine in childhood that is relevant to the patient's problems. Children generally enjoy hearing about the events of their parent's lives that occurred at that time in the parent's childhood that corresponds to the age of the child at the time of the conversation. Such discussions draw children closer to their parents. The same principle holds in therapy. Such revelations, then, can contribute to a deepening of the therapist-patient relationship. As mentioned, a good relationship is crucial if therapy is to be successful. Without it, there will be little receptivity to the therapist's messages and practically no identification with him or her.

Many therapists, especially those with a classical psychoanalytic orientation, may take issue with the freedom with which I reveal myself. They would argue that I am contaminating terribly the therapeutic field and making the patient's free associations practically useless. I am in full agreement that such revelations contaminate the patient's free associations. I am not in agreement, however, that the classical approach is without its drawbacks. It does indeed provide the so-called "blank screen" for the purest projections. However, the acquisition of such information is done in a setting which, I believe, is antitherapeutic. It creates a distance between the therapist and the patient that compromises the development of a good therapist-patient relationship. The patient's thoughts and feelings about the therapist become distorted and divorced from reality. The situation increases the likelihood that the patient will develop delusions about the therapist and will idealize him or her. It will widen the gap between them as the patient comes to view the therapist as perfect. We can love most those whom we know nothing about—but such love is more delusional than real, based as it is on a paucity of information. What is gained in the way of pure free associations is more than counterbalanced, I believe, by the losses of a compromised therapist-patient relationship and the antitherapeutic experience of the patient comparing him- or herself negatively with the therapist. *The Talking, Feeling, and Doing Game* provides the therapist with the opportunity to reveal defects in a noncontrived and nonartificial setting. He or she thereby becomes more human to the patient, and this is generally salutary for the therapist-patient relationship. In addition, my revelations are not those that would compromise my own privacy and that of my family. Even with these restrictions, there is enough that has gone on in my life to provide me with a wealth of potential information for revelation.

I uniformly answer all questions. Some highly defensive children, however, may find it difficult to do so. Sometimes, I will inform such children that failure to answer the question will result in their not getting a reward chip, and this will lessen the likelihood that they will win the game. Some children are motivated by this "threat" and try to respond to the card. On occasion, a child will refrain from answering most cards but still involve him- or herself in the game. Many of these children listen attentively to my responses and, I believe, gain thereby from the game. Although I am working here in a partial volume because I am not getting as much information from the child as is desirable, my knowledge of the child's history and background provides me with enough information to give responses to the cards that are meaningful to the child and pertinent to his or her problems.

The question is sometimes raised about winning and losing when playing therapeutic games with children. *The Talking, Feeling, and Doing Game* obviates this problem. It may not be immediately apparent to the therapist that the main determinant as to who wins the game is *luck*. If each player answers each card, the determinent as to who wins the game is the dice. If a player obtains many high throws, then he or she will reach FINISH earlier and thereby acquire fewer chips. If a player obtains a larger number of low throws, more chips will be acquired when going from START to FINISH. Because low and high throws average out for each player, the number of wins and losses also average out over the course of treatment.

Although *The Talking, Feeling, and Doing Game* was originally devised to engage resistant children in therapy, it has proved useful for less defended children as well. In fact, it has proved to be the favorite therapeutic activity of the children in my practice. Many other therapists have informed me that this has been their experience as well. This therapeutic boon is not without its drawbacks, however. One danger of the game is that it will lure the child (and, unfortunately, the therapist) away from utilizing techniques that are more likely to elicit "deeper" psychodynamic material. Dealing with this material is also important in therapy. Accordingly, the therapist should not injudiciously "respect" the child's wishes to devote the entire therapeutic experience to this technique. The game is generally useful for children over the age of 5 or 6, the age at which they begin to appreciate the give and take structure of board games. At that age, of course, the therapist may have to read the cards to the child (or read along with the child), but this is not an impediment. Whereas *The Mutual Storytelling Technique* and its derivative games are generally not useful above the age of 11, one can get a few more years mileage from *The Talking, Feeling, and Doing Game*. My experience has been that it can be useful up to the age of 14 or 15. Throughout this book I will demonstrate its utilization in the treatment of children with separation anxiety disorder. Many of the cards directly relate to their educational and learning symptoms while others relate to these at a more fundamental level via their drawing the children's attention to some of the central life problems that are at the basis of the psychopathology.

UTILIZATION OF THE PARENT AS "ASSISTANT THERAPIST"

For many years I practiced in the traditional manner and saw my child patients alone. Usually the mother rather than the father was available to bring the child. My procedure was to have the mother bring the child and then sit in the waiting room. However, I did not strictly refrain from involving her in the treatment. I would intermittently bring her in to discuss certain issues with the child, and also had occasional separate sessions with her and/or the father. In my initial evaluation, I would see the mother and father, both individually and together. In addition, during the initial evaluation, I would also have a session or two with the child and the parents together, and even occasionally bring in one or more siblings. However, the basic therapeutic program after the initial evaluation was that the child and I were alone in the room. As is true of most trainees, I automatically accepted as optimum the methods of treatment used by my teachers and supervisors. I believed that being with the child alone was crucial to the development of a good therapist-patient relationship, and that to the degree that I brought third parties into the room, to that degree I would compromise our relationship. In addition, I believed that it was very important to have a confidential relationship with the child, a relationship in which he or she would have the security of knowing that I would not reveal to the parents *anything* he or she told me.

Over the years I became increasingly dissatisfied with this procedure. When something would come up in a session that I thought would be important for the mother to know about (nothing particularly confidential), I would bring her in and, in the last few minutes of the session, quickly give her a run-down of what had happened and then would make some recommendations. Most often this was done hurriedly; however, on occasion we would run overtime because I considered it important that she fully understand what had happened in the session and what my recommendations were. My usual experience was that the mother had little conviction for the recommendations, primarily because she had not been witness to the situation that brought them about. When I started keeping the mothers in the room for longer periods of time, I found that the children generally did not object and, in addition, the mothers had greater conviction for my recommendations because they had been witness to the situations that had brought them about. They not only had the opportunity to observe directly the events that resulted in my suggestions, but they had ample time to discuss them with me in detail. This resulted in their much more frequently and effectively carrying out my recommendations. To my surprise, the children did not express any objections. They had not read the books that I had read —books that had emphasized the importance of my seeing the child alone and the crucial role of the confidential relationship.

General Ways in Which Parents [Usually the Mother] Can Be Useful in a Child's Therapy

Gradually my procedure evolved to the position of informing the parents that they would be my therapeutic assistants in the child's treatment. Recognizing that it would most often be the mother who would be bringing the child, I invited the father to feel free to attend, without any prior notification, any session when he was available. My experience has been that this occurs from 5 to 10% of the time. For ease of presentation I utilize the term *mother* when I refer to my therapeutic assistant. However, it should be understood that fathers are available on occasion to serve in this role. My usual procedure is to have the mother come into the session with the child at the outset, and then to keep her in the room as long as I consider it warranted. This ranges from 5 to 10 minutes to the full session.

The mother can be useful in a number of ways. The younger the child, the less likely that he or she is going to be able to recall many of the important events that occurred since the last session. This is especially the case if the child is seen only once a week. My usual experience is that when I ask a child at the outset what has gone on since I saw him or her last, there is no response. It is almost as if the child were frozen in ice or transfixed in space since the previous session. Knowledge of these events is often vital for the understanding of many of the child's therapeutic productions. The mother, almost invariably, is a ready source of this important information. I have mentioned that the more knowledge the therapist has about the child, the greater will be his or her capacity to respond with a meaningful story utilizing *The Mutual Storytelling Technique*. These stories, like dreams, often relate to important events that have occurred in the day or two prior to their creation. The child is often not in touch with these events, nor will he or she readily provide them. Many mothers, when hearing the child's story, offer these vital data. It is important for the therapist to appreciate that the mother knows the child far better than he or she. Although not trained as a therapist, her hunches about the meaning of a story may be better than the therapist's—regardless of the number of years of psychoanalytic training the therapist has had. In the post-story discussion period, as well, the mother's input can prove invaluable.

In analyzing the dream the mother's assistance can also be invaluable. The child may include in the dream a figure who is entirely unknown to the therapist. The therapist certainly should obtain as many associations as possible from the child. This, of course, is the best way of ascertaining exactly what the dream figure symbolizes for the child. However, most children provide only a paucity of associations to their dream symbols, and the mother's input can be extremely valuable. She can ask the child leading questions about the figure, and she can often be a better interrogator than the therapist because she has some hunches about what may be important. And, when this fails, her specific and direct comments about the dream figure can often provide the therapist with useful information for understanding the dream.

The presence of the mother in the room enables the therapist to observe mother-child interactions that would not have otherwise be seen. The mother's observations of the ways in which I handle the child, especially when he or she is being difficult, can be useful to her in that it provides her with a model for handling these situations herself. (I am not claiming that I always handle every situation in the most judicious fashion. However, I believe that I do so more frequently than most of my patient's parents.)

The effects of parental participation on the treatment are important and may be even more important than the specific way in which a parent can be useful to treatment. Whereas originally I was taught that such participation would compromise my relationship with the child, my experience has been just the opposite. It is hard to have a good relationship with someone who is a stranger, and whose only or primary contact is the monthly bill. Not only is such a situation likely to produce some alienation, but the paucity of contact increases the likelihood that negative distortions and misinterpretations about the therapist will not be corrected. Having the mother in the room provides her with the opportunity to air her grievances, express her resentments and disappointments, ask questions, and so on. This is the best way to prevent or resolve such problems. Both parents' feelings toward the therapist are extremely important in determining what the child's feelings will be. A parent's animosity toward the therapist frequently, if not invariably, will be picked up by the child. If there is a dispute between the therapist and the parents, the child will have a loyalty conflict. Most often he or she will side with the parent. After all, the parents are providing the food, clothing, and shelter; they are the ones who are with the child the remaining hours of the week. The child knows where his or her "bread is buttered," and it is extremely unlikely that the child will, over a period of time, basically support the therapist's position when it is in conflict with the parents'. Accordingly, anything that can improve the relationship between the therapist and the parents is likely to strengthen the tie between the therapist and the patient.

Parental participation can strengthen the therapist's relationship with the parents in other ways. Seeing the therapist "in action" enables the parents to know firsthand exactly what is going on in the sessions. They are not left in the dark about the therapeutic procedure. In the traditional method, parents are ignorant of what is going on, and this can be a source of irritation and alienation. This is especially the case when the parents are paying for the treatment. When they know what they are spending their money for, they are less likely to harbor negative distortions and criticisms. Of course, if the therapist is spending significant amounts of time with traditional play therapy—which is much more *play* than therapy—then the parents may have a justifiable criticism and may reasonably consider themselves to be wasting their money. The techniques that I have thus far described and those I describe elsewhere (1975a) are, I believe, much more *therapy* than play. I believe that one of the main reasons child therapists often hesitate to allow parents to observe them is that they are basically ashamed of what they are doing.

Parents most often feel ashamed of the fact that they are bringing their child for treatment. No matter how much the therapist may try to assuage their guilt, they generally feel that they were at fault. And even though the therapist may initially say to the parents that they did their best and that they should not feel guilty, he or she then proceeds to ask questions that are basically designed to elicit information about what the parents did wrong. And the acquisition of this vital information cannot but entrench and enhance guilty feelings. The facts of the matter are that the parents did make mistakes, or else the child would not have developed psychogenic difficulties. As benevolent as were their motivations, as dedicated as they may have been to the child-rearing process, they were indeed deficient in certain areas and that is why the child is coming for treatment. Platitudes and gratuitous reassurances regarding the inappropriateness of such guilt are not likely to work. One way of genuinely reducing such guilt is to invite the parents to be active participants in the therapeutic process. In this way they become directly engaged in reducing and alleviating the very problems that have brought about their guilt. And the working-together process produces a sense of camaraderie with the therapist which also entrenches the relationship with him or her.

In the field of psychiatry, people like to give labels and names. I am often asked what I call this therapeutic approach. It is not family therapy because it is rare for all family members to be present. In addition, when I do have family sessions, they are primarily during the diagnostic phase. While I do practice family therapy in certain situations, that is not what I am describing here. It is more than parental counseling, which is also part of my therapeutic process, because the parent is actively involved in the child's treatment. The name that I use for the method is *Individual Child Psychotherapy with Parental Observation and Intermittent Participation*. Although this name is somewhat cumbersome, it describes accurately what I do. It focuses primarily on the child and the techniques that I utilize are primarily designed for child therapy. Accordingly, it is a form of individual child psychotherapy. However, there is parental observation in that the parent (usually the mother) observes directly the therapeutic process. In addition, she actively participates to the degree that it is warranted during the session. To date I have not come up with a better name for this procedure.

I wish to emphasize again that the presence and participation of the parents do *not* usually compromise the therapist-patient relationship with the child—although this is what I had been taught, and this is what many still believe. The basic determinant of the relationship between the therapist and the child is their own personalities. A healthy mother does not believe that her relationship with her first child will be significantly compromised by the appearance of the second or third. No competent therapist would advise a parent to have only one child, lest the relationship with the first be compromised by the appearance of a second. No healthy mother strictly excludes the father's presence on those occasions when she is with her child, with the argument that it will compromise her relationship with her son or daughter. It is not the presence of one or a few others in the room that is the primary determinant of the relationship between two people. The relationship depends more on qualities that exist within and between the two of them. Therapists who strictly adhere to the traditional view may be providing the child with an antitherapeutic experience. This view expresses, both explicitly and implicitly, the notion that exclusivity is crucial for a good relationship. This can only engender possessiveness, egocentricity, intolerance for sharing, excessive dependency, and other untoward reactions.

Situations in Which the Parental Presence Is Contraindicated

It would be an error *always* to involve a parent throughout all of the sessions. In my view, this would be substituting one inappropriate therapeutic procedure for another. Those who strictly refrain from parental involvement are providing their patients with what I consider to be a significantly compromised form of treatment. Similarly, those who would strictly adhere to the opposite, that is, insist that a parent be present in every session—throughout the session—are imposing an equally rigid and, on occasion, antitherapeutic treatment procedure. What I am suggesting is that the therapist have the flexibility to tailor each therapeutic program to the particular needs of the patient. Most, but not all, patients do best with active parental participation. However, there are some children for whom the active parental participation is contraindicated. And it is these situations that I discuss here.

First, there is the issue of the child's age. I generally do not treat children below the age of about 4. There is no strict cutoff point at the 4th birthday. There are children who are younger than 4 who are psychologically older than 4, and these may be good candidates for treatment. And there are children who are older (4½, 5, or 5½) who still might not be candidates for direct therapy. But generally, it is around the age of 4 that the average child becomes a potential candidate for a meaningful therapeutic endeavor. Prior to that age my therapeutic focus is primarily on work with the parents, with intermittent interviews with the child, both alone and with the parents. I want to establish familiarity and groom the child for treatment if the counseling does not prove to be adequate to relieve the problem(s).

At about the age of 11, children may start revealing confidences that should not justifiably be communicated to the parents. (As I will discuss later, below that age I do not believe that most children have a significant amount of material that warrants the special confidential relationship so frequently utilized by many therapists.) Also at about the age of 11, many children begin to appreciate that their projected fantasies are revealing of their own problem, and they may become defensive about utilizing such techniques. In fact, children at this age generally consider traditional play therapy approaches to be beneath them. Accordingly, after the age of 11 or thereabout a high degree of parental involvement in the treatment may be contraindicated. Again, there should be no sharp cutoff points here. It depends upon the child's maturity and the nature of the information being discussed.

When an overdependent child is in a symbiotic relationship with an overprotective mother, the therapist would not want to utilize the mother to a significant degree in the therapeutic process. To do so might only entrench the pathology. Such a child needs "breathing space" and the freedom to develop a separate relationship—separate from that which he or she has with the mother. To actively involve the mother in the treatment may defeat this goal. However, this does not mean that the mothers of such children should be strictly excluded from all aspects of the child's treatment. No harm is done, in my opinion, by having the mother come in during the first few minutes of the session in order to apprise the therapist of the events that have occurred since the previous session. In addition, she can be kept in the waiting room to be "on call" should her further participation be warranted. (This is standard procedure for me. I do not support a mother's going shopping or attending to other activities while the child is being seen. I emphasize to her the importance of her being available, at a moment's notice, during the session. And this can only be accomplished by her remaining in the waiting room.) Even when a child is suffering with separation anxiety disorder, some active participation with the mother can be useful. Here again one would not want to keep her in the room for significant amounts of time.

There are some parents who are so psychologically fragile that they cannot tolerate the criticisms and other forms of negative feedback that would come their way during the therapeutic session. This is especially the case for parents who are psychotic or borderline. Such a parent may be so defensive that he or she would not be able to handle many of the therapeutic revelations, even though expressed symbolically. Were the parent to sense the underlying meaning of a hostile symbol, it could be ego debasing and precipitate psychological deterioration. Exposure of such a parent to the child's therapy could be considered cruel and would be likely to alienate significantly both the parent and the child. Any benefits that the child might derive from the parent's presence might be more than offset by the compromise of the therapist-patient relationship that such exposure might result in. In addition, such benefits might also be obviated by the parental psychiatric deterioration and its resultant compromise of parenting capacity. This is not a common situation, but I mention it because it does occur.

There are parents who are extremely hostile, and such hostility might be exhibited toward the therapist. No matter how hard the therapist tries, such parents never seem to be satisfied. No amount of explanation or discussion seems to reduce the hostility. Yet, such parents may bring their children. When they are invited to participate actively in the child's treatment, they may use the opportunity for the collection of ammunition, for example, "Is this what I'm spending all my money on?—to hear you tell those stupid stories?" "How is answering questions about whether or not he touches his penis going to help him obey me at home?" and "My husband is right: psychiatry is just a lot of bullshit!" Such parents tend to "cramp my style" when I am working under their observation and scrutiny. I have the feeling that everything I am doing is going to be used as ammunition against me. Attempts to discuss their negative attitudes have often proved futile. Accordingly, I have found it in the child's best interest to have such parents sit in the waiting room. Although I am deprived of their input, such loss is more than counterbalanced by the enhanced efficiency of the individual therapeutic process with the child. It is the lesser of the two detrimental alternatives. Therapy, like life, often boils down to such a choice. If there were a better option, I would utilize it. So I work under these compromised circumstances.

One might ask the question: "What about the overbearing mother who is always intruding in the child's therapy? Shouldn't she be kept out of the room?" My answer to this question is: "Not so quickly." Let us take, for example, the following situation. I am in session with Jimmy and his mother. I ask Jimmy a question. His mother answers. At that point I consider myself to have a golden opportunity for a meaningful therapeutic interchange—an opportunity that would have not been possible had the mother been out of the room. At that point I will say to Jimmy, "Jimmy, what just happened?" Jimmy may respond, "You asked me a question." And I will respond, "And what happened then?" Hopefully, Jimmy will respond, "My mother answered you." To which I will respond, "Right! And what did you do?" Jimmy may answer, "I didn't do anything." To this I will respond, "Yes, Jimmy, that's right. You didn't do anything. But I believe that you had certain thoughts and feelings when your mother answered my question and didn't give you a chance to answer it yourself. What exactly did you think at the very moment she answered? Exactly what were you feeling at that time?" Here, of course, I will try to get the child to express the thoughts and feelings that he must have had about his mother's intrusiveness. It is generally easier for the child in the therapist's presence. The child recognizes that the therapeutic situation reduces the likelihood that the mother will react with severe punitive measures in the therapist's presence. The child may fear that there will be "hell to pay" when he or she gets home, but the child also knows that there will be at least some protection in the consultation room. If the therapist can encourage such expression during the session and use it as a point of departure for a therapeutic approach to the mother's intrusiveness, it will have served a very useful purpose in the child's treatment.

As mentioned, the richest therapy is that which provides experiences. When the parent is in the room, there is a much greater likelihood that significant experiences will take place. The therapist should view such experiences as golden opportunities, to be grabbed onto and milked to their utmost. They are the most meaningful aspects of the therapeutic process, and they should be cherished. Accordingly, I do not quickly remove instrusive parents from the room. I can conceive of the possibility of a parent being so compulsively intrusive that I would not have the opportunity for such interchanges, and that no living space would be provided the child. However, this has not yet occurred, and I have been successful in utilizing the situations in which the intrusiveness was exhibited as a step toward a reduction of the problem.

This same principle is operative in the more common situation where the child is fearful of expressing hostility toward a parent, hostility engendered by a wide variety of parental deprivations and maltreatment. In a session in which there is the implied therapist's protection the child can be most comfortable in first expressing his or her resentment. Having done so under protected conditions, the child will generally feel more comfortable doing so outside of the session.

I had an experience a number of years ago that demonstrates this point quite well. A boy repeatedly complained to me in sessions that his father insisted that he finish every morsel of food at every meal. His father would be extremely angry at him if he did not eat every speck of food. I asked him if he had expressed to his father the resentment he felt over this. The patient stated that he was afraid to do so. I knew the child's father in that I had interviewed him on a couple of occasions during the evaluative process and, in addition, had seen him on two occasions in joint session with the mother and the child. I knew that he was not as punitive as the patient viewed him to be, and that although he was indeed insisting that the child finish all the food on the plate, he would not have reacted anywhere nearly as violently as the patient anticipated. Accordingly, I felt comfortable encouraging the child to express his resentment. I would not have done so had the father been more punitive. In that case, I would have tried to work more directly with the father himself.

Each week I encouraged the child to express his resentment and told him that I would be asking him in the next session what had happened. Each week he returned with some excuse: "Oh, I forgot to tell him this week." "I was very busy this week." "I had a lot of homework to do this week." I knew that this could go on for months and contribute to the perpetuation of the symptomatology that was a derivative of the pent-up hostility the child was feeling. Accordingly, I had a family session during which I encouraged the child to express his feelings about the mealtime situation. He hesitantly did so and had the *living experience* (again that important concept) that his father did not react as punitively as he had anticipated. We all recognized that he was expressing his anger in a safe situation, with the implied protection of the therapist. However, it was following that session that he became freer to express resentments in other areas and to assert himself more generally. Had I not brought the father into the room, it might have taken a much longer time to achieve this result.

A rarer, but nevertheless very important situation in which the parent's presence is generally contraindicated, is the one in which the parent is suffering with an incurable disease. If the parent is openly discussing the disease, then the parental involvement can be salutary for both the child and the parent. However, if the parent is using denial and other related defense mechanisms as a way of dealing with his or her reactions to the illness, then participation in the child's therapy can be detrimental to the parent. One would not want to have such a parent exposed to the child's working through his or her reactions to the inevitable death of the parent. Such exposure can be cruel and inhumane. Having the parent there will probably lessen the likelihood that the child will reveal his or her true feelings because of the appreciation (depending upon the child's age, sophistication, and intelligence) that his or her revelations may be detrimental to the parent.

The Issue of Confidentiality as It Relates to the Parents' Involvement in the Child's Treatment

Many therapists would take issue with the above concept of child therapy because they believe that the active involvement by a parent(s) would significantly compromise the child's confidentiality, and this they believe is crucial if there is to be meaningful therapy. I believe that such therapists are placing too much weight on confidentiality. The patient is coming primarily for treatment, whether the patient is a child or an adult. The patient is not coming primarily for the preservation of confidentiality. I believe that to the degree that the preservation of the confidential relationship serves the end of treatment, to that degree it should be respected. On the other hand, if it is a choice between confidentiality and doing what is in the best interest of the patient therapeutically, then, I believe, the therapeutic indications should be given priority over the confidences. One must not lose sight of the primary aim of therapy: to do what is in the best interests of the patient. In order to describe my position more specifically, I will consider the confidentiality issue as it pertains to the treatment of the adult, the adolescent, and the child. Although there are differences with regard to confidentiality in these three areas, there are basic similiarities that hold for all three categories.

Confidentiality in Adult Therapy. If the adult is to have a successful therapeutic experience, he or she must have the feeling that the therapist will not disclose to others what is revealed during the course of treatment. Otherwise, the freedom to reveal will be significantly compromised—to the point where therapy may become meaningless. Most therapists would agree, however, that there are certain situations in which strict adherence to the confidentiality may be antitherapeutic. Such is the case when there is a strong suicidal or homicidal risk. Basically, when a human life is at stake, concerns about confidentiality are reduced to the point of being trivial. If the patient is suicidal, it behooves the therapist to enlist the aid of family members and close friends to do everything possible to protect the patient. This usually involves their active participation in hospitalizing the suicidal patient. It would be unconscionable, in my opinion, to "respect" such a patient's request that the suicidal danger not be divulged to the nearest of kin. Similiarly, when there is a homicidal risk, the therapist should do everything possible to warn the potential victim.

When a patient in treatment raises the issue of confidentiality, I will openly state that he or she can feel secure that I will not reveal what is divulged—with the exception of situations in which there is a homicidal or suicidal danger. In most cases, the patient is thereby reassured that confidences will not be divulged because neither of these eventualities seems likely. On occasion, however, a depressed patient will be told that I might divulge the suicidal danger. In such cases I will reassure the patient that everything will be done to avoid such disclosure. However, I inform the patient that there might be an occasion in which I might divulge the suicidal risk, if such divulgence might prove lifesaving. Interestingly, most patients are not upset by this. Some healthy part of them appreciates that they could conceivably "go crazy," and that at such a time they might impulsively commit a self-destructive act that could cause irreparable damage and even death. My position provides reassurance that should such a situation occur some healthy and stabilizing intervention will take place. My experience has been that this is usually reassuring.

In recent years there have been a number of cases in which the litigation has centered on this issue. Psychiatrists were sued for malpractice because they preserved patients' confidences, and there was a resultant suicide or homicide that could conceivably have been prevented. The usual defense was that the therapist was respecting the patient's confidentiality and acting in the highest ethical traditions of the medical profession. Even in former years, I did not subscribe to this view. It is not in the highest ethical tradition of the medical profession to sit by and do nothing when there might be a suicide or homicide taking place. It is in the highest interest of the medical profession to protect human life. Fortunately, the courts and ethical committees in medical societies are shifting in the direction of supporting divulgences in such cases. This is a good trend in my opinion.

Confidentiality in Adolescent Therapy. It is not uncommon for me to have the following conversation with an adolescent:

Patient: Everything I say to you is just between me and you. Right? You'll never tell my parents anything I tell you. Right?

Therapist: Not right.

Patient: You mean you're going to tell my parents everything I tell you?

Therapist: No, I didn't say that either.

Patient: But my friend goes to a shrink, and his shrink told him that everything they speak about is strictly confidential, and his shrink says that he'll never tell my friend's parents anything about what goes on in a session.

Therapist: Yes, many psychiatrists work that way. But I don't. Let me tell you how I work. As long as you don't do anything dangerous, to either yourself or others, you can be quite sure that what we speak about here will be held strictly confidential. I'm in full appreciation of the fact that it's important that you have the feeling that what we talk about is strictly confidential. However, there are certain exceptions. And these exceptions hold for anyone, regardless of age. My policy is the same for all. It's not just for teen-agers. It's the same whether you're 5 years old or 85 years old. The basic policy is this: As long as you're not doing anything dangerous, you can be sure that I won't reveal what you tell me. However, if you're doing something that's dangerous, I reserve the right, at my discretion, to reveal to your family whatever I consider important to reveal to help stop you from doing the dangerous thing. I *may* need their help. What do you think about what I've said?

At that point the patient may ask me to tell him or her what things I would reveal. I will not then provide "food for thought." I do not wish to give the youngster suggestions for various forms of antisocial and/or self-destructive behavior that may not have entered his or her head. Rather, I ask the adolescent to tell me what things he or she might do that might warrant such divulgence. I may then use this as a point of departure for a therapeutic inquiry. However, I do have a "list." It includes: heavy use of drugs (not occasional use of marijuana), heavy use of alcohol, dangerous driving (especially when under the influence of drugs or alcohol), criminal behavior, and for girls, a desire to have an out-of-wedlock child (occasional sexual intercourse is not a reportable item). I also impress upon the adolescent the fact that should one of these dangerous situations be arising, I will not automatically discuss the problem with the parent. Rather, I will exhaust all possibilities of discussion with the patient and the adolescent group before divulging the risk. Usually, such discussions are enough. However, when they are not, the youngster usually knows beforehand that I am going to divulge the information.

There is another aspect of the confidentiality issue in adolescence which warrants comment. The parents have a reasonable right to know whether there is a significant risk of dangerous behavior. When this issue is broached, generally in the initial evaluation, I will tell them that they should know that "no news is good news," that is, that I will divulge dangers to them, and if there are no such divulgences, they can feel assured that no great risks are imminent.

I am fully appreciative of the fact that the adolescent needs a special, separate relationship with the therapist. This is part of his or her developmental need to establish a separate identity from that of the parents. This autonomy is necessary if the adolescent is to grow into an independent, self-sufficient adult. Active participation of the parents in the adolescent's therapy can compromise this goal. However, the goal can still be achieved by some participation on the part of the parents. Occasional joint sessions in which the youngster is seen along with the parents need not interfere with this goal. There can still be a significant percentage of sessions devoted to the adolescent, him- or herself, and the confidential relationship can also serve the purpose of enhancing separation and autonomy. The potential divulgence of a dangerous situation also need not interfere with this sense of autonomy so important to the adolescent's development.

Confidentiality in Child Psychotherapy. By child psychotherapy I am referring to the treatment of children between the ages of about 4 and 11. In my opinion, the confidentiality issue has little if any place in the treatment of most of these children. There are many therapists who will say to such children something along these lines: "Whatever you tell me here in this room is just between you and me. I promise I'll never tell your mother or father what you tell me. You can trust me on that." Many children might wonder exactly what the therapist is referring to. They know of no great secrets that they have from their parents. And this is especially the case for younger children. The parents know quite well that the child is soiling, stealing, lying, truant, and so on. They more than the child are aware of these problems, and it is they who initiated the treatment. So the statement must be confusing and even irrelevant to many children.

In addition, the statement sets up a structure in which there are "we" (the therapist and the patient) and "they" (the parents). "We" *and* "they" can easily become "we" *versus* "they." And this concept can introduce schisms in the family. The family has enough trouble already; it does not need an additional problem brought about by the therapeutic program. The system also impedes open communication. Generally, communication impairments contribute to the development of and perpetuation of psychopathology. The confidential relationship with the child is likely to increase the communication problems of the family. The thrust of the therapy should be to encourage open expression of the issues that are causing people difficulty. A conspiracy of silence usually serves only to reduce communication and defeats thereby an important therapeutic goal.

The therapist should attempt to create an atmosphere in which there is an open pool of communication—an atmosphere in which all things pertinent to the child's treatment are openly discussed with the parents. I do not make any statements about this; I do it as a matter of course. I make no mention of the confidentiality. If the child says to me that he or she does not wish me to tell his parents something, I will get very specific about what it is he or she wishes me not to divulge. Almost invariably it is an issue worthy of being discussed with the parent. Usually, the child fears repercussions that are unreal and exaggerated. Encouraging the child to express to the parent(s) the forbidden material, either in my presence or at home, is usually therapeutic. It can teach all concerned that the repression (unconscious) and suppression (conscious) of thoughts and feelings is likely to perpetuate problems; whereas civilized discussion is the best way to resolve family problems.

There is an aspect of Freud's famous Little Hans case (1909) that is pertinent to my discussion here. During the one joint session that Freud held with Little Hans and his father, Hans expressed some hostility toward his father that he had not previously revealed. I believe that it is unfortunate that Freud did not direct his attention to this in his report of the case. I would speculate that the reason why Hans had not expressed the hostility previously was that he was afraid to do so because of fears of his father's retaliation. However, in the presence of "Professor Sigmund Freud," a man of whom both the patient and his father were in awe, Hans could safely reveal his anger because of his awareness that his father was not likely to react with severe punitive measures in Freud's presence. I suspect that Hans' having had the living experience that his father would react to his hostility in a civilized manner made it easier for him to express his resentments elsewhere. And this, I believe, was a contributing factor to the alleviation of his symptoms. Elsewhere (1972c) I have described in detail this and other aspects of the Little Hans case.

Classical psychoanalysts, in particular, are strict adherents to the confidentiality principle. It is they, more than other therapists, who make it a point at the outset to emphasize to the child that they will respect confidences. It is of interest that Freud did not consider confidentiality to be an important issue in his treatment of Little Hans. Hans' father was the therapist and Freud was the supervisor. When reading the transcript of the treatment, one observes that Hans revealed just about every intimacy one can imagine a child might have: bowel movements, urination, masturbation, interest in observing his mother's toilet functioning, sexual fantasies toward his mother, and so forth. If he were indeed hiding material that a child might be ashamed to reveal, I would find it hard to imagine what such material might be. Little Hans knew that his father was revealing their discussions to Freud. In the one joint session that Freud had with Hans and his father, there was open discussion of these intimacies. Classical analysts often point to the case of Little Hans as the proof that Freud's theories of infantile sexuality, the Oedipus complex, and castration anxiety are valid. Libraries have been written on these theories—which are supposedly proven by the Little Hans case. However, the structure of Freud's therapeutic program is often ignored by the same psychoanalysts. They do not utilize the parents as assistant therapists (as did Freud), and they enter into a strictly confidential relationship with the child (which Freud did not do). In both cases, I believe, they do the child and the family a disservice.

Clinical Examples of the Utilization of the Parents as Assistant Therapists

The way in which a mother served well as an assistant therapist is well demonstrated by the case of a boy whom I will call Jack. He was 6½ when he entered treatment. The chief complaint was stuttering. I consider stuttering to have a strong neurophysiological basis; however, I also believe that psychogenic factors can affect the stuttering in that in tense situations the stuttering is more likely to be worse. Accordingly, my psychotherapeutic approach with such patients is to make every attempt to reduce their tensions in the hope that the benefits to be derived from such reduction will ameliorate the stuttering symptomatology as well. I therefore explore other areas of difficulty, especially those that that may produce tension and anxiety. In Jack's case, such difficulties were not difficult to find. He was significantly inhibited in asserting himself, especially with his father. He was particularly fearful of expressing resentment toward his father and expected dire repercussions for such expression. His father, unfortunately, was very insensitive to Jack. However, he would not have responded with the terrible punishments Jack anticipated. In those situations in which Jack squelched his anger, his stuttering would predictably increase. Jack's anger-inhibition problem was so profound that he was generally viewed as a "model child" by his teacher, parents, and the parents of his friends.

One Monday afternoon (the day is pertinent) Jack began the session with his mother (whom I had learned could be an extremely valuable "assistant therapist"). He said that he had nothing much to talk about and asked if he could draw something with crayons. Suspecting that he had something important to "say" with this medium, I readily agreed. First he drew a blue pond. Then he drew grass and trees around the pond. Lastly, he drew some fishes in the pond and then put down the crayon. When I asked him if the picture was finished, he replied that it was. I then asked him to tell a story, and he stated, "A boy went fishing there, and he caught a few fish." When I attempted to get him to elaborate upon the story, he flatly denied that there was anything more to the story. I told him that I considered him an excellent storyteller, and that I was sure that he could do better. Again, he stated that there was nothing more to the story. When I asked him if there was anything else he could add to the picture, he again stated that the picture was completed. I noted that there were no figures in the picture, either human or animal, and suspected strongly that this had some significance. However, it would have been antitherapeutic to suggest that he place figures in the picture, in that this would have been a significant contaminant to the purity of his fantasy.

I turned to Jack's mother and asked her if she had any ideas regarding the meaning of Jack's picture and "story." She responded strongly in the affirmative, and then turned to Jack and began an inquiry. She first asked him if he recalled what he had asked her on arising the previous morning, which was a Sunday. Jack had no recollection. Upon further urging he did recall that he had asked her to ask his father to take him fishing. She then asked him what her response was, and Jack replied, "You said that Dr. Gardner said that it's a bad idea for you to be my messenger boy, and that if I wanted to ask Daddy something, I should ask him myself." The mother agreed that that was what happened, and then asked him to continue telling what had happened. Jack replied, "I asked Daddy if he would take me fishing, and he said that he wouldn't take me now, but that the would take me later." In the subsequent inquiry by the mother it was revealed that for the next five hours Jack repeatedly asked his father to take him fishing, and the father repeatedly said that he would do so, not then but later. Finally, by midafternoon, Jack's father told him that it was too late to go fishing.

The mother then described how Jack's stuttering immediately became severer. Whereas earlier in the day the stuttering had been relatively mild, it became so bad following this final rejection that Jack was practically unintelligible. And the increased severity was still present when I saw him the following day. The picture and its associated story now became completely understandable. It clearly represented the fantasy that had existed in Jack's mind throughout the previous day. There was a pond that he hoped to visit. The story about the boy who went fishing represented his wish that he were indeed to have gone, but he never did. In the egocentricity of the 6½ year old, if he is not there fishing, then no one is there—thus the conspicuous absence of human figures. In this situation, I decided not to tell a responding story but to use the picture and the associated inquiry with his mother as the point of departure for further discussion.

I then asked Jack what his thoughts and feelings were after what had happened with his father the previous day. Jack denied any resentment at all over the rejection. He reiterated his father's statement that it was really too late in such a way that it was clear that he considered his father's excuse to be justified. I responded incredulously that I could not believe that there wasn't even a little bit of anger over what had happened. In the ensuing discussion Jack did admit to some anger and then we went on to discuss what he feared would happen if he were to express his resentment. I reassured him that his father, although insensitive at times, was not the kind of person who would be as punitive as Jack anticipated. I then suggested a joint session with the father in which the whole issue could be discussed.

In the following session Jack hesitantly and with some fear did express his disappointment over his father's rejection the previous Sunday. The session proved to be a meaningful one, and was the first of a series in which Jack *had the experience* (that word again) that expressing resentment did not result in the terrible consequences he had anticipated. If Jack's mother had not been present in the session, I would not have known what the picture meant, and we would not have then gone on to the series of meaningful and therapeutically useful discussions that focused on issues that were at the core of Jack's anger-inhibition problem.

There is hardly a week in my work with patients that I do not have an experience in which the presence of the mother (and occasionally the father) provides me with information that I would not have obtained had I worked alone with the child. A child with minimal brain dysfunction began drooling while talking with me. Without interrupting the conversation, his mother took a handkerchief and wiped the saliva. The boy continued as if nothing had happened. I interrupted the conversation and asked the mother if this were a common practice. She admitted that it was. Out of this came a discussion of other examples of her overprotectiveness. The experience opened up a whole area that had not been previously known to me.

Concluding Comments

I believe that the traditional practice of seeing children alone while mothers are in the waiting room compromises seriously therapeutic efficacy. My experience has been that children's treatment proceeds much more rapidly when there is active participation by parents. I believe that thousands (and possibly even millions) of hours have been wasted by having mothers sit in waiting rooms reading magazines while their children are being seen alone by their therapists. In many cases such therapy is basically a waste of time. I am referring here to therapy that is primarily play. If the parents are paying for this, they are paying for a very expensive playmate. But even when the therapy is providing the child with a richer experience, it is still not as efficient nor as effective as it might have been if there were more active parental involvement. Throughout the rest of this book, I will be describing the techniques I believe can be useful in the treatment of separation anxiety disorder. Throughout I will be describing also the ways in which parental participation has been useful in these children's treatment.

6

Specific Therapeutic
Techniques

In this chapter I will discuss the details of the specific psycho-therapeutic approaches that I find useful. I will demonstrate the implementation of the therapeutic principles that have been presented in previous chapters. Although some comments will be made with regard to work with the parents, the primary emphasis will be on the therapeutic work with the child. Particular emphasis will be given to the utilization of the *The Talking, Feeling, and Doing Game* and *The Mutual Storytelling Technique* in the therapy of children with separation anxiety disorder.

THERAPEUTIC WORK
WITH THE MOTHER

The likelihood of a school-phobic child being helped by a therapeutic approach that does not actively involve the mother is very small. It is unrealistic to expect such youngsters to give up the gratifications of overdependent status by themselves. As long as the mother continues to be inordinately overprotective, the child is likely to remain overdependent. Unfortunately, the mothers of these youngsters are rarely motivated for treatment. They have little if any pain over their problems, and so are rarely motivated for therapy for themselves. In fact, they view themselves as better than other mothers and usually have the support of their husbands in this regard.

Some therapists try to convince such mothers of the importance of treatment. I personally have not found it useful to try to talk people into the fact that they need therapy. If an individual does not have at least some insight into the fact that problems exist, some pain over the presence of the problems, and some motivation to do something about them, then it is unlikely that therapy will be successful. In addition, trying to convince someone that problems exist generally only increases resistances to the development of insight and motivation. Such an approach, then, is likely to lessen rather than enhance the likelihood that the mother will go into treatment. Some therapists will try to engage such mothers in treatment by encouraging them to enter therapy for the sake of the child. Again, this rarely works. An individual cannot be expected to enter into meaningful psychotherapy in order to help someone else. Again, without insight, pain, and motivation, the therapy is likely to be a sham.

So what does one do with these mothers? Most are willing to come for counseling. Most welcome the opportunity to discuss with the therapist issues that pertain to the child. As mentioned, they are not likely to be receptive to many of the recommendations—especially those that threaten the symbiotic tie. This further limits the therapist's capacity to bring about meaningful change in these mothers. What alterations they make are often related to passive compliance with the therapist's authority and fears that school authorities will take legal action if the mother does not cooperate more in bringing the child to school. As a result of this there is some desensitization on the mothers' part to the separation (as is true for the children) and they may progressively become more comfortable with longer absences. In addition, if they can be helped to involve themselves in other activities, the separations may become even easier. If these can provide ego enhancement they may have less of a need for the esteem-salvaging maneuvers associated with the pathological overprotection of the children.

On occasion, one may be able to engage such mothers in treatment. Generally, these are the mothers whose problems are less severe than those described above who exhibit the typical clinical picture. In the therapeutic work with these mothers a central issue to be focused on should be the compulsion to overprotect the child. These mothers have to be helped to gain insight into the many factors that are contributing to their overprotectiveness. However, it is not simply insight that will help them. Rather, they have to utilize such insights in the service of changing their general life situation so that they need not resort to the overprotectiveness.

One factor that commonly contributes to the overprotectiveness is a deep-seated feeling of maternal inadequacy. When this factor is operative, the overprotectiveness serves to compensate for the feelings of deficiency. At times, these feelings are part of a broader problem in feelings of low self-worth. The mother has selected the child-rearing role as the one that will ensure her gaining the greatest sense of competence and prestige. It is beyond the purposes of this book to discuss in depth the treatment of low self-esteem problems. Elsewhere (Gardner, 1973c) I have described what I consider to be the primary factors operative in producing feelings of low self-worth. When working with such a mother, one has to help her understand the specific causes of her feelings of low self-worth, that is, the particular factors that are operative in producing this symptom in her. The therapist must then try to help her find healthy modes of behavior that are likely to bring about genuine feelings of self-esteem. It is only in this way that she will be able to give up the pathological modes of compensation. She has to be helped to appreciate that her view of herself as a "super-mother" is just one manifestation of this compensatory mechanism and that her denigration of other mothers does not generally stem from deficiency on their part, but from the need to compensate for her own feelings of maternal inadequacy. She has to be helped to appreciate that such deprecation does not genuinely work in bringing about enhanced feelings of self-worth in herself. But this is only one aspect of the maternal overprotection symptom.

Another area that must be focused on in the treatment of these mothers is their hostility toward the child. They have to be helped to appreciate that all mothers have occasional (and even frequent) periods of anger toward their children and that all mothers, at times, may even have primitive death wishes. She has to be reassured, however, that such death wishes are the ways that the unconscious mind manifests hostility, and that it does not really mean that she wants her child dead. Reassuring a mother that such thoughts and feelings are common can contribute to a lessening of the guilt that these mothers often feel over their hostility. In fact, they generally have much more guilt over hostility toward their children than the average mother. In order to assuage such guilt they utilize the mechanism of reaction formation. They have to be helped to gain insight into the fact that each time they unrealistically anticipate catastrophe in the child's life, they are expressing their hostility. However, one must be quick to reassure them that this does not mean that they are loathsome for such thoughts; rather they are merely like other mothers who also have such angry thoughts. They have to be helped to appreciate that the main difference between themselves and other mothers is not that they harbor the hostility, but that they are more guilty over their anger. This is one of the areas in which the therapist's authority is utilized in guilt assuagement. If there is a good relationship with the therapist, then the mother is more likely to accept as valid statements that such anger is common, but her guilt is unusual and inappropriate. If the therapist is successful in this regard, the mother will have less of a need to utilize the mechanism of reaction formation, and this will contribute to her lowered vigilance and overprotectiveness.

The mother has to be helped to appreciate that *her own dependency problems* are also contributing to the child's difficulties. She has to be helped to appreciate that she is very dependent on her own mother. This may be difficult because she may view its manifestations as examples of their closeness. She then has to be helped to see that such dependency is producing insecurities in her children, because this interferes with their viewing her as a stable person in their lives, as someone who can be relied upon for support and guidance. She has to be helped to achieve an independent existence, separate from that of her own mother. These goals may be extremely difficult to reach. The mother may not have had one day in her life in which she did not either see or telephone her mother. Attempts to wean herself from this dependent tie may result in a "cold turkey" reaction. Accordingly, it must be slow but deliberate.

In all fairness to the maternal grandmother, she should be warned in advance about the weaning process. She then may increase pressures on the mother to maintain the tie, and this may complicate the therapy. On occasion I have had sessions with the maternal grandmother, as well, in an attempt to break the symbiotic tie between her and the mother. But if the maternal grandmother is elderly and alone, this may be extremely difficult. More important than the actual proximity between the mother and grandmother is the psychological involvement. For example, if the mother and maternal grandmother live close by, simply suggesting that they move further away from one another may prove of little value. I am not saying that it is of no value at all, only that a strong psychological dependency can exist even though there are great distances between the parties. There are situations in which the mother (and father) may be financially dependent on the maternal grandmother (and maternal grandfather). In such cases it may be even more difficult to break the dependent ties. If the therapist is successful in this regard the mother may have less of a need to gratify vicariously her dependent needs via indulgence of the projected fantasy of herself within the child. As mentioned, when this mechanism operates, it is as if each time the mother indulges the child she is indulging herself via fantasized embodiment of herself in the child. This mechanism is often difficult for therapists to appreciate, and it may be even more difficult for the mother to do so. However, her insight into this psychodynamic pattern is not crucial to its alleviation. Rather, if she can be helped to become less dependent on the maternal grandmother, she will have less need for this mode of gratification for her dependent needs.

Many of these mothers have sexual inhibition problems. And they are often comfortable with husbands who have similar difficulties. Accordingly, there may be little if any marital friction in the sexual realm. Their children, especially their sons, may serve as sexual surrogates. I am not referring here to the utilization of the children for overt sexual gratification. Rather, I am referring to their use as sources of physical and sensual gratification that the mother may not appreciate has sexual connotations. Through cuddling and hugging, the mother may gain enough physical gratification to satisfy her low level of sexual need. In some cases, the male child becomes a husband surrogate in other ways. This is especially the case as the child grows older. A son may serve as her companion in social situations with very hazy lines drawn as to whether the child is accompanying her as a child or as a peer. Such mothers are generally threatened by an egalitarian heterosexual relationship and more comfortable with the "sexual partner" being younger and more dependent. A control element is obviously operative here as well.

The therapist has to help these mothers become less guilty over their sexual feelings and experience the rewards of a mature relationship with an adult peer in both the sexual and nonsexual realms. The possibility of this occurring within the marriage is enhanced if the husband is also motivated for therapy and/or marital counseling. If he too does not grow up and become comfortable with and desirous of an egalitarian sexual/physical relationship with a woman, then the woman's growth and development will result in an incompatability that may not have existed previously. If the husband fails to achieve this higher level of egalitarianism, then a mother may seek to achieve it outside the marriage. Obviously, it is preferable that this be accomplished within the confines of the marriage, for the sake of both the parents and the children.

Just as the child with separation anxiety disorder has to be helped to grow up in all areas of life, these mothers have to be helped to do so as well. In fact, if the mothers still remain children psychologically, it is not likely that the children themselves are going to mature adequately. Many of these mothers lead very isolated lives and have never developed any extradomestic interests or skills. Encouragement to enter into such areas is often an important part of their treatment. This may involve going back to school and/or entering into vocational training. Such involvement exposes them to a more rigorous life outside the home and, over time, may help them grow up. Competence in the extradomestic realm may serve to reduce the effect of another contributing factor to maternal overprotectiveness. Specifically, many of these mothers do not want their children to grow up because the child-rearing process is the only realm in which they can gain a sense of importance. They dread the prospect of the so-called "empty nest syndrome" when they will have no children to rear. Keeping their children in an infantile dependent state is their way of forestalling the day when this will occur. To the degree that the therapist can facilitate such education and training, to that degree will this contributory element be reduced.

Obviously, this part of the therapeutic program is not likely to take place in a short period. Obviously, also, this may take longer than the child's treatment. If the mother's treatment continues beyond that of the child's (the preferable course in many cases), then the therapist has a greater opportunity to provide input into the mother's maturational process. If, however, she discontinues when the child experiences alleviation of his or her difficulties, then the therapist may not be able to fully achieve this goal. However, even then, some progress along this path may have been made. Central to both the therapeutic and the maturational process for the mother is learning better how to deal effectively with the fundamental problems of life. This was described earlier in this book in my discussion of the ways in which symptoms arise and are alleviated. In this approach, the patient must be helped to learn to deal better with the inevitable problems of life with which we are all confronted and to consider options for resolution of such problems that may never have been considered. And such learning is central to the mother's maturation.

THERAPEUTIC WORK
WITH THE FATHER

As mentioned, the fathers of these children are often extremely passive and dependent on the mothers. On occasion I have seen fathers who have been aware that their wives are overprotective and have complained about the mother's "spoiling" the children. However, even in these cases they have submitted to the mother's compulsion to overprotect the child. These more insightful fathers will welcome the therapist's support for their position: "You see (to mother), that's what I've been telling you all along. You're spoiling him sick." "Doctor, I knew that she was indulging him, but she never listened to me."

More often, however, the fathers have little insight into the mother's overprotectiveness. Furthermore, the very passivity they exhibit in their relationship with the mother results in their not being powerful therapeutic allies for the therapist. In family therapy the therapist should ascertain which members of the family may serve in this capacity. Such healthier members are not only likely to be of assistance in the family sessions per se, but can be relied upon to monitor healthier behavior outside of the therapeutic sessions. They are almost like the therapist's delegates or traveling assistants. The fathers of school-phobic children, unfortunately, rarely qualify for this role. Furthermore, their dependency on their wives is so great that they may find anxiety provoking the therapist's attempts to get them to be more self-assertive with their wives and to interfere with their overprotectiveness.

Last, my experience with active involvement by fathers in the treatment of most children has been limited. Although I actively enlist their involvement and welcome their attending any session that they are available (without necessarily giving me prior notice), the bulk of the work is generally done with the mothers. And children with separation anxiety disorder are no exception in this regard. However, because it is the mother-child diad that is generally the central element in the pathology, the limited involvement of the fathers does not prove to be a serious compromise, although compromise it still is.

THERAPEUTIC WORK WITH THE CHILD

Regarding the individual work with the child, I generally begin each session with the mother and child together. This is my usual procedure. For the child with separation anxiety disorder, however, I try to confine such joint meetings to a very short period at the outset of the session. As described elsewhere (1975b) I generally work closely with parents and refer to my primary therapeutic approach with most children as *individual child psychotherapy with parental observation and intermittent participation*. However, there are certain situations in which close ongoing work with the parent and child together is contraindicated. Children with separation anxiety disorder are in this category. To keep the mother in the room with the child throughout most of the session is to perpetuate the very psychopathology one is being asked to alleviate. This does not mean, however, that one should not allow the mother to step into the room at any point. She can be a valuable source of information and provide other forms of therapeutic assistance. Accordingly, the compromise I make is to have the mother in the room during the first few minutes in order to get any information that she may be able to provide me. After that, she is asked to sit in the waiting room, and I generally do not have further contact with her during the session. This does not preclude, however, my bringing her in for a few minutes from time to time if the situation warrants her joining us.

As mentioned, the main goal of treatment is not simply to get the child back to school. It is to help the child reach the level of independence and maturity that is appropriate for his or her age. I try to help the child mature in *all* areas of functioning whether they be in the home, neighborhood, or school. I try to help him or her learn better ways of adapting to the realities of life. Like Roberta, the child needs to be helped to grow up in all major areas of functioning. If, for example, the child complains about being picked on by other children, I will discuss in great detail the various ways that children can handle those who try to scapegoat them. I am a strong proponent of the ancient wisdom: *knowledge is power.* Any enhanced knowledge or competence that I can help my patients gain is likely to be therapeutic. The child has to be helped to appreciate the fact that cowards and brave people are quite similar in that both suffer with initial fears. Cowards submit to them; brave people force themselves to tolerate their fears while doing the thing that they know they must do. It is to be hoped that this advice will not only contribute to the child's tolerating school anxiety but, even more important, tolerating the inevitable fears that we all suffer when we enter new and strange situations—especially those that are challenging. I try to help the child tolerate and squelch the fears most people have of asserting themselves and encourage proper and appropriate self-assertion. I try to help the child appreciate that the discomforts associated with such self-assertion are generally far outweighed by the benefits to be derived from such expression. In general, I encourage direct expression of thoughts and feelings as a preferable method for dealing with the problems of life.

Regarding the central anger problem, this may be harder to deal with in treatment. I consider it to be more deeply repressed (both for the patient and the mother) and not as accessible to conscious awareness and discussion. However, this does not preclude my providing messages (via *The Mutual Storytelling Technique, The Talking, Feeling, and Doing Game,* and other techniques described previously) that relate to the problem. I try to help reduce children's guilt over their anger. I attempt to do this by advising them that angry thoughts and feelings toward parents are normal and that all human relationships are mixtures of both loving and hateful feelings. I may point out that the main difference between them and others is that they feel worse about their anger than others, but they do not differ from others in regard to the presence of angry thoughts and feelings. I also attempt to help them appreciate that angry thoughts and feelings cannot bring about their realization.

I take the opportunity to express my views on the subject of magic and include the fact that thoughts are not magical and cannot make things happen in the world outside of the head in which the thoughts reside. For a younger child I might in the course of play therapy make comments along these lines: "This boy was really angry at his friend who had now become his enemy. He was so angry that he wished him dead. But no matter how hard he wished him dead, he still didn't die. No matter how hard he strained his brain, the other kid still stayed alive. He kept wishing it for hours—praying that it would happen—but nothing happened. At least a thousand times he said, 'I wish he was dead'—but the other kid still remained alive. The enemy didn't feel any pain and he didn't even suffer with a scratch—even after all those thoughts and wishes. It took all that to help the boy realize that *thoughts can't harm!*"

I try to help children appreciate that all human relationships are ambivalent, including the relationships children have with their mothers. I try to help them alter internal dictates regarding anger, dictates such as: "Good boys never get angry at their mothers or fathers," "Curse words are bad—especially if you think them about your mother or father," "Thoughts can make things happen," "Thinking a bad thing is just as bad as doing it," and "Good people have no bad or angry thoughts."

On a number of occasions my therapeutic work has resulted in the child's returning to the school, to the point where there has been minimal if any anxiety. I have accomplished this without significant delving into the underlying anger problems. The parents and the child at that point have raised the question as to whether further therapy is warranted. It may come as a surprise to some readers that I will not place great pressure on the parents to keep the child in treatment at this point. The primary factor that motivates people to remain in treatment is psychological pain. When there is less pain there is less motivation for treatment. In child therapy, the pain is rarely the child's. Most often it is the parents'. When the child is attending school and both the parents and child have learned to tolerate the separation, they may have little pain. One might argue that recurrence is likely if the underlying problems—especially those around anger—are not worked through. My experience has been that this is not the case. Perhaps the anger theory (and that's basically what it is) is wrong. Perhaps the desensitization program was all that was needed. Or, perhaps the messages I have provided regarding the central anger issues have operated to bring about the change without there being much conscious awareness on the part of the child and the parents that these factors have been operative in bringing about the therapeutic change.

The therapist who pressures the parents into keeping the child in treatment because of the belief that the underlying problems have not been worked through (especially if "working through" must include conscious awareness of underlying psychodynamics), may be doing the family a disservice. The increasing resentment caused by such pressure may compromise the relationship between the parents and the therapist. And this can often interfere with the progress of the treatment. In addition, it may "sour" the child on therapy and therefore reduce the efficacy of the treatment. Such souring may make it more difficult for the child to re-enter treatment if it is warranted in the future. These experiences with the anger elements in the separation anxiety disorder lend support to my original speculation that the conditioning element may be more important than the anger factor in bringing about the separation anxiety disorder. Further experience in the treatment of this disorder should enable us to make more definitive statements regarding this issue.

The Use of The Talking, Feeling, and Doing Game

As is true for so many other clinical disorders, *The Talking, Feeling, and Doing Game* can be useful in the treatment of children with separation anxiety disorder. I present below the kinds of responses I would provide in a typical case.

Question: Say something that tells about a feeling—any feeling at all.
Response: The feeling I'd like to talk about is *fear.* Everybody has fear. There is no one in the world who is comfortable with everything. Even the bravest people have fears. Even the most courageous people have fears. The difference between a brave man and a coward is often not very great. The brave man and the coward are both afraid. But the brave person forces him- or herself to do the thing that is frightening; the coward just runs away. The brave person knows that it is impor-

tant to do the thing, even though he or she is afraid. The brave person fights the fear and does the thing anyway. And each time the person does the thing he or she finds out that the frightening thing is less fearful. And that is true bravery! Do you fight *your* fears or do you give into them? Do you let your fears get the best of you, or do you get the best of them?

The response, of course, encourages desensitization and conscious control. It also provides an important message for just about everyone.

. . .

Question: What is the worst thing a boy can say to his mother?
Response: Before answering this question, I think it's important to point out the difference between *thinking* something and *really wanting it to happen.* Most people have terrible thoughts enter their minds. This doesn't mean that they really want these things to happen. It just means that thoughts come into our minds that we really cannot control. These thoughts are different from really wanting the thing to happen.
  A boy, for example, might have a thought that he wished his mother were dead. It's not that he really wants his mother to be dead. In fact, it would probably be the worst thing that could happen to him if his mother really died. To have the thought on occasion is probably normal; but to *really* wish it to happen is probably not. Some kids feel very guilty about such normal thoughts. They think that it's terrible to have a thought or a wish sometimes that a mother might die. The wish is one kind of normal thought, and most kids have such wishes once in a while. That doesn't mean that they *really want* such mothers to die. It's just that the wish pops into their heads. That's normal if it happens once in a while. The problem is feeling guilty or bad about an occasional wish. Having the thought or wish once in a while is normal. Have you ever had such thoughts or wishes that your mother might die?

The response directs itself to the deeper problem of many children with separation anxiety disorder, namely, the repression of their anger because of the guilt they feel over their hostility. As mentioned, my experience has been that many, if not most, of the children I see with separation anxiety disorder do not reach the point of analyzing this underlying hostility or dealing with the issue directly.

It is probably dealt with indirectly via the fact that there is less to be angry about when the therapist is successful in reducing the mother's overprotectiveness. Also, helping the child to become independent raises self-esteem and also reduces anger. With less anger, there is less anger to be repressed, there is less guilt, and there is less anger to be projected.

. . .

Question: What do you think about a girl who sometimes wished that her sister were dead?

Response: It's perfectly normal to have the thought and wish *sometimes* that one's sister were dead. It's understandable that when two sisters live together they sometimes get under each other's skin. It's reasonable to expect that from time to time they'll get very angry at one another and at such times might even have thoughts that involve the other sister's dying. It doesn't mean that the girl actually *wants* her sister dead; it only means that the thought can come to mind, and that's perfectly normal. There's a big difference between having a *thought* about a sister's dying, having a *feeling* about a sister's dying, and actually *really wanting it to happen.* Of course, it would be a bad thing to really want it to happen over a long period of time. But to have such a thought once in a while is perfectly normal. In fact, the child who never has such a thought about a sister or brother dying probably thinks such thoughts are terrible and won't let them come into his or her mind.

As was true for the previous vignette, my comments here attempt to reduce guilt over the expression of hostile thoughts and feelings. For such a child I might also attempt to disspell the illogical element involved in the notion that a hostile thought can bring about its own realization. I attempt this with a comment such as:

There are some people who believe that an angry thought can actually make the thing happen. The girl we were talking about might have the idea that if she had the thought that her sister would die, she actually would die. This can't happen. No matter how hard a girl may wish her sister dead, the wish itself cannot make it happen. She can wish it all day and all night and it still would not make her sister die. Even it if happened that her sister died, it could have not been from the thought. Thoughts cannot make things happen; only things can make things happen. Wishes cannot make things happen; only actions can make things happen. Things only happen when people *do things;* they don't happen just by people thinking things. So this girl is normal if she has wishes that her sister were dead. She has a problem, however, if she thinks that the wish can make that happen. She has a problem if she feels bad about herself for thinking that such thoughts make her a terrible person and might cause her sister to die.

. . .

Question: A boy's friend leaves him in order to play with someone else. How does the boy feel? Why did the friend leave?

Response: Actually, the friend who left the boy wasn't such a good friend. Let's call the boy Jim and the one who wasn't such a good friend Bob. Now Bob only played with Jim when there was no one else around. Although they were the same age, Jim was immature. By that I mean he used to act like a younger kid. He got that way because his mother always babied him. His mother never let him do the things that other kids his own age were doing. He was a "mama's boy." His mother didn't let him swim in the deep water when other kids his age were already diving off the diving board. His mother didn't let him ride his bike, even on his own block. She was always hanging out the window to watch him. She never let him sleep overnight at other kid's homes. And because of these things he didn't act his age. So Bob only played with Jim when there was no one else around.

On this day, when Bob and Jim were playing, Fred came along. Fred was also their age. As soon as Bob saw Fred he lost interest in playing with Jim. The two of them went off to climb in some rocky places where Jim wasn't allowed to go. They weren't really dangerous, these rocks, it was just that Jim's mother didn't want him to play there. Jim was very sad.

At this point, I might ask the child with a separation anxiety disorder, whose anger towards his mother is repressed, how Jim felt besides being sad. If the child cannot get in touch with his or her anger I might say:

Well, in my story he was also mad. He felt *sad and mad.* He was *sad* because his friend left him and he was *mad* because his friend left him. He was also very angry at his mother because she watched over him so much and prevented him from doing so many things.

In the subsequent discussion I would try to help the child express the angry feelings that he or she must also feel in such a situation. The aim would not simply be to get such feelings expressed. I would try to reduce the feelings of guilt that have contributed to their repression. I would discuss specifically what the child anticipates would happen if he or she were to express anger. And I would go into the various changes that might be brought about if the child were to express this resentment. Of course, in such situations the child might not be able to rely very much on the father for support, but he or she might be able to rely on the therapist to support the request and demands for greater opportunities for growth and independence. It is very difficult to motivate children who strive toward alleviation of overdependency problems because there is so much gratification from the overprotective mother. It is in the area with friends, however, that the child may suffer embarrassment and pain over the overdependency. And it is here that the therapist should attempt to motivate the child to strive toward becoming more independent and mature and thereby reduce the teasing and taunts to which immature children are often subjected.

Clinical Example -- David

This clinical example demonstrates how *The Mutual Storytelling Technique* and *The Talking, Feeling, and Doing Game* can be useful in the treatment of children with separation anxiety disorder. David was referred at the age of 9½ by his pediatrician. Three months prior to referral, he began suffering with abdominal pains. These began about one month after starting the fourth grade and were so severe that he had not attended school during the six weeks prior to my initial consultation with him. Thorough medical evaluations by three pediatricians revealed no organic cause for his difficulties, and he was therefore referred for consultation.

David was the youngest of six children, the older siblings ranging in age from 23 to 16. Accordingly, there was a 6½-year hiatus between David and his next oldest sibling. During the five years prior to the initial consultation, the older siblings began to leave the household, one at a time. The oldest three had already left the home and the fourth, an 18-year-old sister, was starting to apply to college. In addition, his 16-year-old brother (the fifth of the siblings) had already left the home three years previously for six months as an exchange student in Europe. The family was a tight-knit one, and these losses were painful for David.

Of pertinence to David's disorder was the fact that there was a strong history of appendicitis in the family. Four of his five older siblings had had their appendices removed and appendicitis was under serious consideration during David's hospitalization. However, absolutely no evidence for appendicitis was found. David's father was a highly successful businessman who enjoyed significant prestige in his community. The family members considered themselves paragons of what a family should be. In such an atmosphere the expression of deficiency was strongly discouraged as were crying, depressed feelings, profanity, and any other manifestations that were considered to be deviant. Lastly, David's new teacher had the reputation of being unusually strict and David found this particularly difficult to handle.

During the initial interview I concluded that David was suffering with a   separation anxiety disorder. In his case it was not so much separation from his mother that was painful, but the progressive and predictable loss of his older siblings who were serving as parental surrogates. It was as if David had seven parents: mother, father, and five significantly older siblings. As they progressively left the home, he felt increasingly alone and fearful about the loss of his various protectors. The closeness of his family intensified the problem. Had there been a looser family involvement he might not have been so anxious. Furthermore, the family pattern in which everyone was required to present a facade of perfection and imperturbability made it extremely difficult for David to express the anxieties, anger, and depression he felt over these losses. Lastly, the family history of appendicitis provided a model for excused withdrawal. Others were seen to get extra attention and affection in association with this illness, and that probably served to give David the idea that he could enjoy such extra protection by the utilization of the symptom. Of course, the abdominal complaints themselves might also have been a manifestation of his tension and anxiety. During his third session, while playing *The Mutual Storytelling Technique,* the following interchange took place.

Therapist: Good afternoon, boys and girls, ladies and gentlemen. Welcome to Dr. Gardner's Make-Up-a-Story Television Program. We have a new guest on our program today. Tell me how old are you?
Patient: Nine.
Therapist: Nine years old. What grade are you in?

Patient: Fourth.

Therapist: Fourth grade. Okay, now, let me tell you how it works. On this program we invite boys and girls down to see how good they are in making up stories. Now it's against the rules to tell a story about anything that really happened to you or anyone you know. The story must be completely made up from your imagination. It can't be about anything you've seen on television or read in books. Then, when you've finished telling the story, you tell the lesson or moral of the story— what we learn from the story. As you know, every good story has a lesson or a moral. And, of course, the more exciting the story is the more fun it will be to watch on television afterwards. Now, when you've finished telling the story, you tell the lesson or moral of your story. Then I'll tell a story and we'll talk about the lesson or moral of my story. Okay, you're on the air.

Patient: It can't be from a book?

Therapist: No, it can't be a story from a book. It has to be completely made up in your own imagination.

Patient: There's this man and a woman, and they lived on top of a huge rock. And they had 16 children and they couldn't find another room. They only had one room.

Therapist: Okay, so there's one room for 16 children. Uh huh.

Patient: And they were all running around and making so much noise that they didn't know what to do. So they called their friend who was really smart . . .

Therapist: So they couldn't handle all the kids? Is that it?

Patient: So the man said if they had any lobster pots. And they said "yes, 16." And he asked them to get the lobster pots. . . .

Therapist: This is the friend?

Patient: Yeah. So he took the lobster pots on his bicycle.

Therapist: He took the 16 lobster pots on his bicycle?

Patient: Yeah, to his home and then at home he got some candy and rope and then he rode back and climbed up to the house, and then when he got up to the house, he said, "Hello . . ." So he tied the lobster pots outside the windows. He had 16 pieces of candy and he put all the candy he had in them.

Therapist: In the lobster pots?

Patient: Yeah, and then the children ran to get their candy . . . and then they jumped into the lobster pots and ate the candy. And the children stayed in the lobster pots.

Therapist The children stayed there?

Patient: These were big lobster pots. They even had dinner there.

Therapist: They even had dinner there? Who served them?

Patient: The mother and father.

Therapist: So they had more room . . . is that it?
Patient: Yeah.
Therapist: Uh huh. Okay. Is that the end?
Patient: That's the end.
Therapist: Lesson?
Patient: Some people will do anything just to have some privacy.
Therapist: Who's having the privacy there?
Patient: The mother and the father . . . they would do anything just to have
    some privacy.
Therapist: And what did they do to the children?
Patient: They just lived with them.

I considered this story to represent well the patient's situation
with his family. Although his family consisted of six children, he
symbolizes it with a family of 16 children. In either case the number
is large and both figures share the numeral 6. The story enabled
David to gratify his fantasy of entrapping his siblings in such a way
that they could not leave the house. Each window contains a lobster
pot into which a sibling can be lured with candy. There the child is
trapped and cannot flee or leave. Ostensibly, the parents do this in
order to provide themselves with some privacy. If that were indeed
their motive, they could have allowed all the children to leave the
house in such a way that there was little if any link or tie to the home.
Accordingly, I considered this reason to be a rationalization. It is the
opposite to what the parents *really* want: entrapment of the children
in the home. Of course, it is not the parents who want this; it is David
who attributes this desire to the parents to serve his own purposes.
The story also reflects some ambivalence about closeness with his
siblings. On the one hand, he wants them close enough to be seen
and ever present (thus he traps them in lobster pots). On the other
hand, he puts them outside the window, thereby providing him with
a little distance and breathing space (a little privacy after all). With
this understanding of David's story, I related mine.

Therapist: I see. Okay, now as I said, when you finish telling your story,
    I'll tell a story and we'll talk about the lesson and moral of my story.
    Now, my story will start off like your story, but different things hap-
    pen in my story. Okay?
        Once upon a time there was a family and this family consisted of
    a mother and a father and 16 children . . . a big family . . . and they

lived in one room. Now everyone was getting kind of edgy . . . living on top of one another and things like that.

And finally they decided to consult a friend of theirs who was very wise. And they said to him, "What do you think we can do about this?"

And the father said, "I have an idea. I think maybe I ought to get lobster pots . . . and put candy in them and put them outside the windows and then they'll go into the lobster pots and then there will be less people around the house and I'll have more room."

And the wise friend said, "Well, look, how old are some of your children? What are their age ranges?"

He said, "Well, they range from very little ones to very big ones."

And the friend said, "Well, aren't the big ones getting ready to leave soon? . . . go off on their own and become adults?"

And the father said, "Well, it should happen pretty soon."

So the wise friend said, "Well, I think that the problem will solve itself as the older ones grow up and leave the house. I think that you want to hold onto these kids too long. If you're going to put them in lobster pots and have them hanging around the house, that tells me that you want to hold them back and keep them in the house forever and not let them grow up and become independent, self-sufficient adults."

And the man of the house realized that the wise man made sense. And he said, the man of the house said, "However, the young ones are going to miss the older ones terribly and maybe we ought to try to keep those older ones there for the young ones' sakes."

The wise friend said, "It isn't fair to the older ones. The younger ones have to accept the fact that the older ones are going to be going. They may feel lonely but you know, they have one another. And they also have other friends they can make."

And the father said, "What about the youngest one? When the other 15 leave, what's going to happen to him?"

The wise man said, "Well, he'll be old enough by then to have his own friends. He'll still have time with the older ones. He'll go and visit them and they'll come to visit him. It's not like they're lost forever. He'll still have some time with them. He'll speak to them on the phone. And then he can make his own friends. He can still be with you people, his mother and father. So it's not the end of his world that he doesn't have that many people around. So . . .

Patient: So they just let them grow up?

Therapist: They let them grow up and then what happened to the younger ones?

Patient: Then they . . .
Therapist: Are they sad?
Patient: I guess so.
Therapist: Uh huh. What happened to them? Anything happen to them?
Patient: I don't know.

It is a well-known principle in treatment that if the therapist is going to attempt to take something away from a person, he or she does well to try to find some reasonable substitute at that point. Even the suggestion that the substitutes be provided at some time in the future is generally not as effective as recommending substitutes in the present. Accordingly, although I recommended in my story that the younger ones resign themselves to the fact that the older ones inevitably are going to leave, I provide definite substitutive gratifications. I recommend that the younger ones involve themselves with one another. The patient still had one younger sibling in the home and so this recommendation was applicable. I also suggested intensified relationships with peers as another way of obtaining compensatory gratification. Lastly, I reminded David that one can still have frequent and meaningful contacts with older siblings even though they are living outside the home. Telephone conversations and visits are still possible and the awareness of this can help assuage the sense of loneliness one might feel after one's older siblings leave the home. At that point I attempted to engage David in a conversation to ascertain whether he appreciated on a conscious level any relationship between my story and his own situation. As mentioned, I do not consider it crucial for the treatment of the patient to have such awareness. What is important is that the message "gets through" and I'm not too concerned whether it is received on the conscious or unconscious level, on the direct or the symbolic level. This is the conversation that ensued.

Therapist: Well, do you think this story I told you has anything to do with you? Has anything to do with your situation?
Patient: Ah, yes.
Therapist: In what way? How?
Patient: My brothers and sisters have gone away.
Therapist: How many brothers and sisters did you have?
Patient: Six . . . 5.
Therapist: Five besides yourself. And what are their ages? How old is the oldest? What are their ages?

Patient: Sixteen, 19, 20, 22, and 24.

Therapist: Uh huh. How many live in the house now?

Patient: Not counting when they go to college?

Therapist: Right. If they're off at college, let's consider them out of the house.

Patient: Two.

Therapist: Two. You and . . .

Patient: My brother, Bart.

Therapist: Who is 16? And what year in high school is he?

Patient: Sophomore.

Therapist: Sophomore? So he still has a couple more years at home?

Patient: Uh huh.

Therapist: Uh huh. Now, how does the story I just told relate to yours?

Patient: It's like me. My brothers and sisters are going away.

Therapist: Uh huh. And how do you feel about accepting that fact?

Patient: I think I can.

Therapist: You think you can?

Patient: Yeah.

Therapist: Does it upset you a lot?

Patient: Not a lot.

Therapist: Do you think being upset about them has anything to do with your stomach? With your cramps and your going to the hospital?

Patient: No. I don't think so.

Therapist: Do you think *your* story has anything to do with your problems or the situation with your brothers and sisters?

Patient: No.

Therapist: I do. I think it has something to do with it. In your story, you put them in cages and keep them around the house. Isn't that right? In your story the mother and father's friend put the boys and girls in cages . . . lobster pots . . . they're kind of cages, aren't they?

Patient: Yeah.

Therapist: And they keep them around the house. They don't go anywhere. They're kind of trapped into staying around the house. I think your story says that you would like to have your brothers and sisters trapped around the house.

Patient (appearing incredulous): Not really.

Therapist: You don't think so. Do you think your story has anything to do with you?

Patient: No.

Therapist: Do you think *my* story has anything to do with you?

Patient: Just a little.

Therapist: Just a little. Okay. Well, anyway, the important thing is that if brothers and sisters stay around the house too long, they don't grow up.

Patient: Yes.

Therapist: And they have to grow up and they have to leave and the other kids left behind have to make friends with others, and it isn't the end of the world.

Patient: Yeah.

Therapist: That's the main message. It's not the end of the world when your brothers and sisters leave. You still have other people ... other friends. And you can still get in touch with your brothers and sisters too, and still see them. Okay, do you want to watch this for a little while?

Patient: Okay

Therapist: Do you want to have your mother come up and see it?

Patient: Okay.

As can be seen, the patient did not gain too much insight into the relationship between his story and mine. Nor did he have much insight into the relationship between his story and his situation. There was some appreciation of some superficial similarity but basically he was unappreciative of the various relationships. He did, however, listen with interest to my story, and I believe that the message got through.

Nine days later, by which time David had already started to exhibit clinical improvement, we played *The Talking, Feeling, and Doing Game* during the session. The following interchanges took place:

Therapist: Good Afternoon, ladies and gentlemen, boys and girls. Today is Thursday, the 13th of December, 1979, and our guest and I will be playing *The Talking, Feeling, and Doing Game.* We'll be back with you when we start reading the cards.

Therapist: My card says "A child has something on his mind that he's afraid to tell his father. What is it that he's scared to talk about?" Well, this boy was angry at his father. His father was doing certain things that were really bothering him and he was so angry that dirty words came into his mind about his father. He was real scared to say that to his father. He had the idea that it was a terrible thing even to think dirty words about one's father. He felt guilty and bad and he thought that he really shouldn't be thinking these angry thoughts and these dirty words about his father. And that's why he was scared. What do you think about that?

Patient: I don't think he should feel guilty if he feels that way, but you shouldn't feel that way about your parents.

Therapist: Well, what about thinking dirty words about his father?

Patient: He really shouldn't do that. . . . It's dumb. Sometimes you can't help it, but you should try not to think things like that about your parents.

Therapist: Do you want to know my opinion about that?

Patient: What?

Therapist: My opinion is that it's normal to even have the worst kinds of words come to your mind about your mother and your father when you're angry. That it's not a good idea to say those words. It's a good idea to say words that are *more polite.*

So, for instance, let's say a kid is angry with his father and he thinks in his mind, "I think he's a shit" or something like that. I don't think it's a good idea for the child to *say* that. What I think he should do is say, "Well, you know I'm very angry at you, Dad, because of such and such." You understand?

Patient: Yeah.

Therapist: But the important thing is do you think that it's a terrible thing that such a thought comes to his mind?

Patient: But he couldn't really help it.

Therapist: Right! Those are things that come to mind when you're angry at somebody.

Patient: Yeah.

Therapist: The thing is, is it wrong for him to have those thoughts?

Patient: No. He can't really help it.

Therapist: That's right! You really can't control thoughts that come to your mind. Okay. You get a chip for that one.

As mentioned, David's family was somewhat uptight with regard to deviating ever so slightly from what they considered to be the behavior of the model family. The expression of profanity was very much outside their scheme of things. This was just one manifestation of the family's emotional inhibitions. My aim here was to loosen David up somewhat and make him more comfortable with the primitive expression of anger that is bound to extrude itself into conscious awareness from time to time in the vast majority of individuals. When introducing my comments, I asked the patient, "Do you want to know my opinion about that?" This is a common way in which I introduce what I consider to be healthier modes of adaptation or more salutary ways of dealing with a situation. My hope is that the patient will give credibility to "my opinion." Clearly, the better the relationship the therapist has with the patient, the greater the likelihood there will be receptivity.

Patient: My card says, "What do you think of someone who sucks his thumb like a baby?" (Patient pauses.)

Therapist: Well, what do you think of people who do that? Anybody, any age.

Patient: When they're young, they just like to do that.

Therapist: Uh huh.

Patient: They like to suck their thumbs when they're babies.

Therapist: Yeah. When you're a baby, that's the time to suck your thumb like a baby.

Patient: Yeah

Therapist: And when you're your age . . . how old are you now?

Patient: Almost 10.

Therapist: Almost 10 . . . when you're 10, you act like a 10-year-old. You know, there are some 10-year-olds who want to act like babies. You know that?

Patient: Yeah, sort of.

Therapist: Well, one thing about a baby is that when a baby gets a little upset about something, he cries and wants his mother to take care of him. He whines and doesn't want to do the things he's supposed to. Do you know that? Do you think you do a little bit of that?

Patient: Uh huh.

Therapist: In what way?

Patient: Uhhh. . . . What do you mean . . . in what way?

Therapist: That you acted like a baby . . . that you didn't act like a 10-year-old? Anything happen to you recently where you didn't act like a mature boy of 10?

Patient: Yeah, I think so.

Therapist: What?

Patient: Ummmm. I just remember . . . I had a fight with my brother. And my mother told us to stop, and I got mad.

Therapist: I can think of another thing you're doing that's like a baby. These stomachaches you're having. You know, these pains you have when you're scared about school and some other things, you know?

Patient: Uh huh.

Therapist: Instead of saying, "Well, I have to go to school and it's not pleasant, but you have to go and do things even if you don't want to." You're kind of babying yourself, you know? You say, "I have stomachaches; I don't want to go to school." And your mother lets you stay home from school. Do you think that's acting like a baby a little bit?

Patient: I guess so.

Therapist: You know there are times when you have to do things you don't
like, because it's important to do them even though you're uncomfortable. When that happens, babies don't want to do these things. They
want to stay home from school, stuff like that. But bigger people know
that you have to do things you don't like to do. Okay, you get a chip for
that.

Here, I directly confronted the patient with how immature he
appeared by using stomachaches to avoid an anxiety-provoking situation. I am a firm believer in the old aphorism: "It's not what you
say, but how you say it." If there is a good relationship with the
patient *and* if the therapist's motives are genuinely benevolent, then
the patient is likely to tolerate even the most painful confrontations.
I believe that this was the situation here. Although it was early in
therapy, I believed that the patient had a good relationship with me
and was receptive to what I was saying. Clarifying for the patient
how he or she looks to the world is an important part of the therapeutic process. The old idea that "your best friends won't tell you"
does not speak well for one's "best friends." An even better friend
than the aforementioned "best friend" will tell you in a benevolent
way for your own good. And this is what a therapist should be.

Therapist: My card says, "Make believe you're doing a sneaky thing."
Okay, let's make believe that I'm in school . . . that I'm some kid in
school—and let's say I've missed school and I'm behind in work. What
I do is . . . the teacher's giving a test and I'm looking over somebody's
shoulder at his paper and copying his paper. And then what happens
is when the test grades come back, I get a good mark, but I don't feel
too good about it. Why is that?
Patient: Because you didn't do your work. You didn't do the work yourself.
Therapist: I would have felt much better if I had gotten that mark by knowing the stuff. When you do something like that you may get a good
grade—and that makes you feel good—but you know in your own
heart that you really didn't deserve it, right?
Patient: Uh huh.
Therapist: So, that's one of the reasons why it really doesn't pay off to be
sneaky about things. Okay, I get a chip. What's your card say?

The patient had informed me that he had on occasion looked
at other children's papers during tests. This was especially the case
after his long absence from school. My usual approach in such situa-

tions is to avoid comments that would imply that what is being done is loathsome or sinful because it goes against rules set down by higher powers. Rather, I focus on more mundane aspects of the situation. Here, I focused on the lowered sense of self-worth that comes from knowing that the grade one has received was undeserved. I may also focus on the fact that without mastery of the subject one is deprived of the advantages of competence. I may also direct my attention to the thoughts, feelings, and reactions of classmates who have observed the copying. The game continued.

Patient: "Say something bad about your mother." My mother smokes a lot.
Therapist: She smokes a lot. How much would you say she smokes a day?
Patient: I really don't keep track.
Therapist: Is it more than a pack, would you say?
Patient: She smokes . . . I see her smoke cigarettes a lot but I don't know if it's a different cigarette or the same one.
Therapist: I see. And how do you feel about her smoking?
Patient: I think she can't help it, because it's a habit, but I just want her to try to stop.
Therapist: You know, I have a difference of opinion from you with regard to people's habits and their not being able to control them. I think that habits may be hard to stop, you know, but people have a certain amount of control over their habits. So, it's hard to stop a habit, I understand that, but she has some control over it. Does her smoking bother you? That's the question.
Patient: Yes.
Therapist: How, in what way?
Patient: It hurts my throat a lot, and I don't want her to get sick.
Therapist: Okay, so there's two reasons. It hurts your throat a lot, and you don't want her to get sick. Okay, now when she smokes, and let's say it hurts your throat a lot, do you say anything to her?
Patient: Only when it hurts my throat a lot.
Therapist: What do you say to her?
Patient: "I wish you'd stop smoking because it's really bad for your health, and I also don't like being around when you do smoke."
Therapist: So, what does she say?
Patient: "I can't help the habit, but I'm trying to stop."
Therapist: But, does she continue to smoke? And does it bother your throat?
Patient: Sometimes. Not always. It does when a lot of smoke comes out.
Therapist: As I understand it, you tell her it bothers you, but she still continues to smoke, right?
Patient: Yeah, but she tried a lot harder to . . . stop.

Therapist: But she still continues to smoke even though it bothers you.

Patient: Yeah. Both my father and mother are trying to stop.

Therapist: What can you do if they're smoking or one or the other of them is smoking and it bothers you, and you say to them, you know, that smoke bothers me. What can you do?

Patient: Go off to another place, to another room.

Therapist: Well, that's one thing.

Patient: I could always suggest that there are things like cigarettes that are bad for your health.

Therapist: There are two parts to it: it's bad for her health, and it's also something that bothers you. It bothers you.

Patient: Uh huh.

Therapist: Now, I understand that you're a child and they're adults and you don't have that much power and control over them, but I'm wondering whether you're expressing enought of the resentment... do you know what resentment is?

Patient: Yeah.

Therapist: What is resentment?

Patient: A hatred of something...

Therapist: I think that "hatred" might be too strong a word...maybe something you don't like very much. And I'm wondering whether you're expressing enough resentment over their smoking.

Patient: Sometimes I do. It causes a lot of resentment.

Therapist: What happens?

Patient: They just say they really can't help it and they wish they could stop.

Therapist: What I was saying, my main point is that sometimes expressing resentment can get something changed and sometimes it can't, but I don't think you're expressing enough resentment. Perhaps you could...even though you're 9, you're still a human being and still have rights to clean air, clean breathing space, and not to have smoke pollution in your lungs. And I think that my suspicion is that you're not speaking up enough. Maybe they would then do something different like smoke in another room or something like that.

Patient: I can try that but smoking is also bad for your health....

Therapist: You may not be able to change their smoking in front of you, but you certainly can do more things to try to change it.

At the beginning of our interchange about David's parents' smoking, his inclination was to excuse their habit as uncontrollable. My comment that people have some control over their habits was not merely made with regard to his parents; I hoped that it would have direct implication to David with regard to his separation anxiety disorder. A certain amount of conscious control is necessary if a child is to help him- or herself with this problem, specifically, control over the fear of attending school and the ability to tolerate the fear.

David had brought up two reasons for his objecting to his parents' smoking: 1) it's bad for their health and 2) it bothers him. As can be seen, I focused on the second reason because I considered it far more important with regard to David's treatment. Although I recognized fully that he is a child in the house (and the youngest of six at that) I still believed that there was certainly room for self-assertion on his part. There is often significant overlap between self-assertion and the expression of resentment. And this was the case here. He was resentful over the fact that his parents' smoking habit caused him significant discomfort. However, he was frightened of expressing his resentment. Here, I encouraged him to do so. And this brings us to an extremely important therapeutic point. There are therapists who believe that the mere expression of anger and other feelings is in itself therapeutic. I believe that this is a somewhat simplified view of the therapeutic process. The expression of emotions such as anger is merely the first step in their proper utilization. One must direct the anger to the situation that is provoking it in the first place in the hope that such expression will remove the noxious stimulus. Otherwise, one is just "screaming in the wind." There may be a little cathartic value to such expression, but it is usually short-lived and does not ultimately deal with a recurrence of the provocation.

Sometimes, such expression helps and the noxious stimulus is removed. At other times, such expression is not successful in removing the source of provocation. In the latter case, the patient must be helped to make a reasonable number of further attempts. When these still fail, then alternative measures have to be considered, the last of which should be resignation. When helping children in this process I often refer to the last chapter of my book, *The Boys and Girls Book About Divorce* (1970c, 1971c) where I quote Fields' Rule (after W. C. Fields): "If at first you don't succeed, try, try again. After that, if you still don't succeed, forget it! Don't make a big fool of yourself."

Such direct self-assertion can be a therapeutic benefit with regard to underlying anger inhibition problems that may be contributing to the child's separation anxiety. By becoming more comfortable with direct expression of anger, the child is less likely to repress it and deal with it via the mechanism of reaction formation. As discussed previously, this mechanism is central to the process by which the child wants to be ever at mother's side in order to be reassured that some feared calamity will not befall her. These indirect ways of reducing guilt over anger most efficiently bring about therapeutic change. I am not in agreement with those who believe that the insight route to bringing about the alleviation of this kind of problem is the most efficacious. I believe that more indirect approaches that deal with issues that are of emotional charge to the patient at the time are more likely to be efficacious. They are less anxiety provoking and less theoretical and intellectual.

The game then continued.

Therapist: My card says, "A girl was listening through the keyhole of the closed door of her parents' bedroom. Her parents were talking and didn't know she was there. What did she hear them saying?" Well, this girl had two older sisters and an older brother. She was the fourth child, and her mother and father were talking about having another baby, and they were discussing the question of whether they should have a fifth child or not, and that's what she heard them saying. Now, what do you think the girl was thinking when she heard that?

Patient: She was probably thinking that... probably thinking happy thoughts about having a little brother or sister and probably trying to encourage them....

Therapist: Why would she want to have another brother or sister?

Patient: Because there'd be more people around.

Therapist: Uh huh. Well, some kids like to have a lot and some kids feel, "Oh, boy, no more, wow! I've got three already in this house..."

Patient: Lots of people think that. But if the mother and father want to have another baby that's good, too.

Therapist: Well, that is certainly one way of looking at it. Now, let me ask you this question. Do you have any problems at all about brothers and sisters?

Patient: I don't think so.

Therapist: How many brothers and sisters do you have?

Patient: Five...

Therapist: And where do you stand in age?

Patient: I'm the youngest...

Therapist: You're the youngest. How many are living in the house at this time?

Patient: Well, there's my brother and my two sisters who already left the house. And my other sister's just started to go to college now.

Therapist: How do you feel about her going away?

Patient: I don't think about it. I don't know.

Therapist: How does that make you *feel*?

Patient: Sad . . . I guess.

Therapist: Are you very sad about it?

Patient: No . . .

Therapist: And who's next?

Patient: My brother, Bart. He's in high school.

Therapist: And what year is he in?

Patient: Sophomore in high school.

Therapist: Sophomore . . . So how much more time does he have around the house?

Patient: Two more years.

Therapist: And what do you think about his leaving. He's a sophomore, he's in the tenth grade . . . What grade are you in?

Patient: Fourth

Therapist: Fourth grade. So he's six years older than you. So you're going to have about six years when you're going to be the only kid in the house.

Patient: Uh huh.

Therapist: What do you think about that?

Patient: I don't know.

Therapist: Think about it. . . . What do you think about that?

Patient: I wouldn't be as happy, because I wouldn't have any brothers and sisters to play with.

Therapist: So what are you going to do?

Patient: I'm going to play with my friends.

Therapist: Were you worried about that when you first came here? When you first used to come?

Patient: Ummm. No, not really.

Therapist: Not really? You weren't worried about that at all?

Patient: Not *not* at all. . . .

Therapist: A little bit?

Patient: Yeah.

Therapist: What was the main worry you had?

Patient: That it wouldn't be as much fun having no brothers and sisters to play with. I'd miss them a lot and everything. But it also wouldn't be as bad because I would have friends coming . . . you know . . .

Therapist: That's the important thing. That you have your own friends your own age, and that your life can be very rich with others. Also, you still have them. You still have your brothers and sisters. They like you.

And they'll be in touch with you and you'll be visiting them, but you'll have your own life . . . your own friends.

Okay, let's see, I get a chip for that. We're going to have to stop this game now. Let's see . . . I guess I win . . . I have five. What do you have?

Patient: One left.

Therapist: Okay, do you want to watch this for a while?

Patient: Okay.

The patient's desire that his parents have more children is atypical. For most children the advantages of more playmates are far outweighed by the disadvantages of the diminished parental attention that the appearance of siblings brings about. For David, however, "the more the better." Rather than continue on a theoretical discussion regarding whether it is good for there to be more children or fewer children in a home, I switched directly to David's situation with regard to the departure of his siblings. As can be seen, by the end of the interchange, he volunteered the two compensations that I had previously provided: 1) he could gain gratification by playing with peers and 2) he can still have contact with his siblings, even though they are no longer living in the home.

One week later, by which time there was further significant clinical improvement, we once again played *The Talking, Feeling, and Doing Game*.

Therapist: Good afternoon, boys and girls, ladies and gentlemen. Today is the 20th of December, 1979, and I'm happy to welcome you once again to Dr. Gardner's television program. Our guest and I are playing *The Talking, Feeling, and Doing Game* and we'll be back with you when it's time to answer a question.

Patient: My card says, "Make believe you're sleeping." (Patient imitates sleeping.)

Therapist: Okay, good, you get a chip for that. Now, you can get another chip if you can make up a dream that you're having while you sleep.

Patient: That I'm getting a toy that I've really wanted for a long time. A remote-controlled car.

Therapist: A remote-controlled car. Did you get it?

Patient: Yes.

Therapist: Okay, you get another chip for that. My card says, "Tell a secret to someone." (Therapist whispers in patient's ear.) Your're not scared anymore to go to school. Right? You used to be scared. Right?

Patient: Uh huh.

Therapist: Why do you think you're not scared anymore? What's your guess? Do you have any idea at all? Do you think that it might have had something to do with coming here?

Patient: Maybe ... yeah ... I think so.

Therapist: What about coming here might have ...

Patient: I don't know.

Therapist: Try to figure it out. See, I get a chip for having told a secret, and you can get one or more chips for giving reasons why you're not scared anymore.

Patient: Well, I went to another classroom and got the teacher I like a lot.

Therapist: So, one of the reasons why you didn't want to go had to do with that teacher that you had. Okay, you get one chip for answering that. Now, any other reasons why you're not scared anymore?

Patient: I think that's about it.

Therapist: Okay. Did we talk about any other things here while you were coming to see me that might have made you less scared?

Patient: I don't know.

Therapist: Can't think of anything else?

Patient: No.

Therapist: There are all kinds of things that we talked about. What did you learn here? Did you learn anything special here that you didn't know before ... that you didn't realize before?

Patient: You shouldn't be scared of something ... if you don't know it's really going to happen.

Therapist: Okay. What else?

Patient: You should talk with the family ...

Therapist: What did you talk about with your family?

Patient: Things about when people go away ... and you should accept that.

Therapist: Were you afraid that something would happen before?

Patient: A little bit.

Therapist: What were you afraid of?

Patient: Accepting that they are going.

Therapist: Did you accept that before?

Patient: Yeah, but not as much before I went here.

Therapist: Is there anything else we spoke about here?

Patient: No.

Therapist: Did we talk about showing anger? Did we say anything about that?

Patient: Yes, we spoke about anger and we shouldn't hold it in.

Therapist: Okay, were you holding in your anger with anything?

Patient: Yes, when I got mad at my brother and things ...

Therapist: What would you do in the past?

Patient: I'd sort of say nothing and hold it in.

Therapist: What are you doing now?

Patient: I'll call him a name or something.

Therapist: Did you learn anything about names or dirty words?

Patient: It's worse to hold stuff in than to say these words. That you shouldn't be disrespectful with your parents, but if you have to, you can.

Therapist: Have you been doing that?

Patient: Well, not much, but I do say the word "jerk" or something.

Therapist: What kind of word wouldn't you use?

Patient: Damn.

Therapist: Anything worse than that?

Patient: Fuck.

Therapist: Fuck. That's hard for you to say, huh?

Patient: Uh huh.

Therapist: Do you think that that's the worse possible word you could say?

Patient: You could say them together and that's the worst.

Therapist: What words together?

Patient: The two words.

Therapist: Say it, which two words?

Patient: Damn and fuck.

Therapist: Uh huh. That's really bad, huh?

Patient: Yes.

Therapist: But is there a place to use those words?

Patient: Yes, I guess like in front of certain people you shouldn't use them.

Therapist: When you say certain people whom are you taking about?

Patient: My parents.

Therapist: Right. That's not a good idea to use those words in front of parents. What if you're angry at your mother and father, what's the best thing to do?

Patient: Not say anything . . . just say "okay" . . . try to accept what they're doing, because it's the best thing for you.

Therapist: Suppose you're *really* angry about something they do, what do you do then?

Patient: I just don't think you should use words like that to parents, and you shouldn't get angry at them.

Therapist: I have a different suggestion about that. Let's say that you're really angry about what they're doing. You should tell them, but you should use words that are more polite.

Patient: Yeah.

Therapist: Then what can happen?

Patient: They can change it.

Therapist: That's a possibility! And then if they don't change it, what happens then? Suppose they don't change?

Patient: At least you tried something.

Therapist: Right! At least you can say you tried. Okay, you get another chip because you answered questions about that. Okay, whose turn is it now?

I used the card "Tell a secret to someone" to transmit a message about the patient's having overcome to a significant degree his fear of going to school. I used the question as a point of departure for an inquiry designed to ascertain how much insight the patient had into his therapeutic change. His first response related to his having talked his parents and school administrator into changing his teacher. There was every reason to believe that the teacher he was assigned was stricter than the one he wished to transfer to. Although I predicted that this was not likely to make a significant difference, the parents, as a manifestation of their overprotection, convinced the principal to change David's teacher. There was some alleviation of symptoms following the transfer but, as I had predicted, the anxieties did not disappear.

In the ensuing interview, it was clear that the patient had little conscious insight into other issues that we had focused on. As mentioned so often previously, I do not consider this to reflect a therapeutic deficit. I believe that most of my important messages get through at the symbolic level, and this may or may not be associated subsequently with conscious insight. Accordingly, I suggested other factors that might have contributed to therapeutic change and got as much mileage out of discussing these factors as I could. However, there were some factors that the patient brought up himself. As can be seen, the bulk of the discussion focused on the anger issue and the interchange is typical of the kind I engage in in an attempt to alleviate anger inhibition problems in children. The child's attitude about the use of profanity can be useful in assessing the depth of an anger inhibition problem. And the therapist's judicious utilization of such terms can serve as a model for the child's proper use of them as well.

Patient: It's my turn. "Make believe you're diving into water." (Patient imitates diving and makes diving sounds.)

Therapist: You dive?

Patient: Mmmm.

Therapist: You do or you don't?

Patient: I do.

Therapist: You do. How long have you been diving?

Patient: Since I was 6.

Therapist: How did you feel when you first dove?

Patient: I was scared at first, but I really liked diving, so I just dove in and got better and better.

Therapist: Yeah. That's how it's like with a lot of things. You're scared at first about doing something new or different, and then after you do it awhile, you get less frightened. That's how it is with a lot of things. There are some people, however, who do a very foolish thing. When they're scared of something, they stay away from it entirely, and they just don't want to have any scary feelings. They don't want to do new things. They lead very boring lives. Do you know what I mean by that?

Patient: Yeah.

Therapist: What do I mean by that?

Patient: They rarely try anything new. They won't try anything.

Therapist: They run away from fear.

Patient: A few weeks ago, my friend jumped up on a tree limb and I was riding on his bicycle. He sometimes jumps up and tries to catch the tree limb and swing on it. At first I was a little scared of doing it, but I jumped up and caught the tree limb and I liked it.

Therapist: Sure, if you didn't do that, you would have been deprived of all that fun.

Patient: And then I did that at school, and I tried it and I really liked it.

Therapist: Sure, that's a good idea. Okay, you get a chip.

As can be seen, the patient volunteered descriptions of incidents in which he overcame his fears by conscious control. First, he described diving into water and then jumping up on a tree limb. In both cases I took the opportunity to reinforce his courage.

Therapist: My card says, "Make believe you're doing something that makes you happy." Well, one of the things that makes me happy is giving speeches and lectures in front of people. I travel around from time to time and give such lectures. And I remember years ago when I first started to lecture, I was very honored that people invited me and wanted to hear me, but I was scared, you know. I had to get up there in front of all those people and think, "I wonder if I'll make a fool of myself. I wonder if they'll think what I'm saying is funny or stupid or something like that."

And then, after I did it awhile, I realized that that didn't happen. You know, of course, there's always somebody once in a while who would think that what I said wasn't reasonable or that it was wrong or stupid, and sometimes I would learn something. Sometimes what I did say was kind of foolish, but most often I found that the things I had to say people thought were pretty good. They agreed and thought I had something important to say. They liked what I said. They liked what they heard and that made me feel good. And I was glad that I had swallowed the lump in my throat. You know what I mean? And as time passed, I became less and less scared so that now I'm hardly ever scared. I'm not zero scared. You know?

Patient: I know.

Therapist: I don't think I'll ever reach that point. I'll always be a little bit scared when I get up there in front of all those people.

As mentioned, I believe it is psychotherapeutically contraindicated for a patient to believe that a therapist is free from inappropriate psychological reactions. Such a belief can only widen the gap between therapist and patient and contribute to the latter's feelings of low self-worth as he or she compares him- or herself unfavorably with the therapist. Accordingly, the therapist should reveal in a non-contrived way occasional deficits that are proper to reveal in the course of the therapy. Of course, if the therapist's are profound and frequently exhibit themselves, then the question should be raised as to whether the patient should be seeing such a therapist. If, however, they exist in mild degree, then the revelation can be beneficial. Here, I used lecture anxiety to provide the patient the opportunity to hear about an area in which I occasionally have felt insecure. I am not claiming that my reactions here are pathological; I am only claiming that they reveal human weakness and common fear.

My other reason for providing this response was related to the hope that the patient would thereby feel more comfortable with his own fears. Knowing that his therapist has experienced such fears can help the patient feel more comfortable with his. Most patients cause themselves additional difficulty by viewing themselves as loathsome for having their symptoms. This only provides them with an additional and unnecessary burden. I hoped that my talking about my fears in a matter-of-fact way would help the patient become less embarrassed about his.

Patient: "What do you like to daydream about?" Well, that I could get something new ... something I wanted ... like a toy. That's what I like to daydream about getting.

Therapist: What particular kind of a toy?

Patient: A remote-controlled car.

Therapist: You really have that on your mind.

Patient: Yeah.

Therapist: How many days is it till Christmas now?

Patient: We're not going to be here at Christmas; we're going away.

Therapist: You're going away. Do you think you're going to get that?

Patient: Well, I was with my father when he got it. I got to see it.

Therapist: Oh, you got to see it? They have already gotten it, I see. So, you're just dreaming about that.

Patient: I'll get it on Christmas or the next day.

Therapist: Uh huh. Now, tell me something. Since you answered that already before to another card ... you know ... you talked about a toy or something like that before. I'd like you to give me another answer. I'm sure you daydream about things other than that car.

Patient: About what I'd be when I grow up.

Therapist: Okay, and what do you daydream about that?

Patient: I daydream that I'd be a stuntman.

Therapist: A stuntman? Okay. Any thoughts about that?

Patient: I'd just like to do that. It'd be adventuresome.

Therapist: That's adventure, let me tell you. Does it scare you to think about that kind of thing?

Patient: Yeah, but then they try things and it gets easier and easier.

Therapist: That's right! But also you learn *how* to do it so it becomes less dangerous. And every time you practice it, it becomes less dangerous, because you know exactly what to do so that you protect yourself from being harmed.

Patient: Yeah.

Therapist: What's another thing that makes things less scary? When you know about them. The more you know about things, the less scary they become. Did you know that?

Patient: I think so.

Therapist: Like being a stuntman. The more you know how to do stunts, the more you practice the art and the skill of doing stunts, the less scary it becomes because you are dealing with something you know and when you deal with it, it becomes less dangerous, so that you aren't as scared. Do you see that?

Patient: Yeah.

Therapist: Can you repeat what I just said, because it's a very important point. I want to be sure you understand it.

Patient: That when it is hard to do something ... like someone going on a tightrope or something ... then it gets less and less scary because you're more confident that you've practiced and things.

Therapist: Right. Okay, you get a chip.

In response to the question the patient first spoke about getting a remote-controlled car. After getting as much mileage as I could out of that response, I reminded the patient that he had already spoken about a remote-controlled car in response to a previous question. Accordingly, I did not accept the answer and then required him to provide me another response. Such stringent adherence to the rules of the game provides me with the opportunity to stretch out the child's answer and derive more information from it.

He then spoke about daydreams of being a stuntman. I immediately viewed this to be a counterphobic fantasy in that it served to deny his fundamental fear of danger. Rather than analyze this, I used the topic to focus on two aspects of overcoming fear: 1) desensitizing oneself by the exposure to the feared situation and 2) gaining knowledge of the feared situation. Although talking about stuntmen, it is clear that I was addressing myself to the patient's school phobia as well as other fears that he had.

Therapist: "What do you do very well? Make believe you are doing that thing." Well, one thing I do well is write. I write books and articles and things like that. So, I'll make believe I'm writing here . . . writing, writing . . . but you know, I didn't write very well just like that.
Patient: Practice.
Therapist: Practice, right. It took a long time. When I first started to write, I couldn't write well. I really didn't start to write well until I was in my thirties . . . something like that. I didn't think I had any particular talent or skill in that area but then I started to write some things, and people were interested in it, and then I started to write some more. I learned a lot from the editors. Do you know what editors are?
Patient: Yeah, they read what you write and correct it and publish it.
Therapist: They don't just publish it. They go over the grammar and the punctuation before it's published. And I watched carefully what they had to say and where the corrections were. Some of them made me feel kind of bad, you know? When I made a stupid mistake or things like that. But what happened is that over the years I learned a lot of things from them even though I wasn't a kid in school, you know? I still found that there were a lot of things I didn't know about grammar, punctuation, spelling, and things like that. And even though I felt bad at times, as time went on, I made fewer and fewer mistakes, and I was glad that I had learned from those mistakes. Okay, I get a chip.

Again, I tried to lessen the gap that forms between therapist and patient when the latter comes to view the therapist as omniscient and omnipotent. By telling patients that I learn from others can make it easier for them to learn from others and can help them become more comfortable with their own deficits. This was especially important for David because his family was so perfectionistic. Admission of defect was not part of the family scheme of things and by my doing so I hoped that I would serve as a model for *his* doing so as well.

Patient: "Show what you would do if you were turned into your father." I'd tell a lot of jokes.
Therapist: Does your father tell a lot of jokes?
Patient: Uh huh.
Therapist: So, let's see. Make believe you're doing that.
Patient: I don't know any good jokes.
Therapist: You don't know any good jokes? Not at all?
Patient: No, not really.
Therapist: Shall I tell you a joke?
Patient: Okay.
Therapist: I'll tell you a joke about a guy who goes to the doctor and the doctor says, "What the trouble?"
   And the man says, "Oh, doctor, it's my hearing. It's getting worse and worse." He says, "Doctor, it's getting so bad I can't even hear my own farts."
   So the doctor examines him and the man then gets dressed and the doctor says, "Take one of these white pills three times a day."
   And the man says, "Will these pills make my hearing better, doctor?"
   And the doctor answers, "No, but it'll make your farts louder."
Patient: (laughs)
Therapist: Like that one?
Patient: Yeah!
Therapist: Okay, you get a chip for that one, right?
Patient: Yeah.

As I had done previously, I used the patient's card as an opportunity to tell an off-color joke. My hope was that this would make David more comfortable with such humor under appropriate circumstances. In his uptight family, there was little place for humor containing profanity. My hope was that my own use of such humor might make the patient more comfortable with it as well. I believe that in the short time I had with this patient, I was successful in this regard.

Therapist: Okay, good. My card says, "What do you think about a boy who
   sometimes plays with his penis when he's alone?" That's my question.
   I saw you make a face when I read that one.
Patient: It's sort of weird.
Therapist: You think it's weird?
Patient: I guess so.
Therapist: Do you want to know my opinion about that?
Patient: Yeah.
Therapist: My opinion is ... Remember, it says "when he's alone." It
   doesn't say "when he's with other people."
Patient: Yeah.
Therapist: I think that to do that when you're alone is a personal, private
   thing. There's nothing wrong with that. But to do it in front of other
   people ... a person like that would be out of it ... out of touch with
   what's acceptable in society. You know what I mean?
Patient: Uh huh.
Therapist: You're not supposed to do things like that in front of other
   people. But I think it's perfectly fine when you're alone. Think so?
Patient: Mmmm. (partially convinced)

As might be expected, the patient was somewhat horrified
about the card. When the patient's view is diametrically opposed to
my own, I generally do not confront him or her directly with my
opposing view. I often will ask the patient if he or she wishes *my*
opinion on the subject. Most often the response is in the affirmative.
I do not present it in such a way that the idea is conveyed that the
patient is "wrong" and that my view is "right." Rather, I try to present an alternative view for the patient's consideration. I believe that
this approach is far less likely to bring about defensive reactions,
denial, avoidance, and other mechanisms for maintaining the pathological position.

Again, this was not a subject that was discussed in this patient's
family. My discussing it in a relaxed fashion served, I believe, to
make David more comfortable with this issue. My hope here was to
decompress the subject. One might wonder how my response relates
to the patient's presenting symptom of separation anxiety. I believe
it relates insofar as any fear of expression of thoughts and feelings
contributes to the patient's primary symptomatology. Symptoms do
not exist in isolation. Their psychodynamics are not narrow and
linear. Rather, the psychodynamics are broad and contribute to the
formation of other symptoms as well. Accordingly, anything that

can contribute to the alleviation of other psychogenic symptoms is likely to be salutary for the presenting symptoms. This approach is consistent with the concepts I have about the origins and development of psychopathology described in Chapter Four.

Therapist: My card says, "What's the most disgusting thing a person can do?" I would say one of the most disgusting things a person can do is to foul up their lives. Someone who just goofs off; doesn't learn anything; doesn't learn how to do something; doesn't learn how to be a person who grows up on his own and can function in the world. You know what I mean? Somebody who becomes a bum or lazy... someone who doesn't ever learn how to do anything or accomplish anything. That's kind of a wasted life.

Patient: Uh huh.

Therapist: I think in order to accomplish that you have to work at it; you've got to do things at times you don't want to do; but most people think that it's worth it in the end. Did you ever go down the street and see a bum on the street.

Patient: Well, sometimes in New York.

Therapist: Yeah, in New York, sometimes. And that's a sad thing and I think that's pathetic. It's tragic for these people, and it's kind of disgusting, too.

Patient: Uh huh.

Therapist: Okay, I get a chip.

Prior to his initial consultation, the patient had missed three weeks of school and was not particularly upset about what he had missed. The gratifications he was deriving from his illness and the extra attention and affection he was gaining from it were so great that he was blinding himself somewhat to its effects on his education. Although he was now back in school on a full-time basis, I provided this response to help him appreciate the importance of commitment to the educational process and the disadvantages and even suffering that may result when one neglects it. Although this response may be considered to be in the "heavy medicine" category, I believe that such dramatizations often have more "clout" than milder examples. Our dreams—which may be an important source of useful information—often follow this principle. Our heritage of fables, myths, and legends would be another example.

Patient: "Say something good about your mother." My mother is very, very nice. She does nice things for me.

Therapist: What are some of the nice things she does for you?

Patient: She helps me with my homework.

Therapist: Does she help you in such a way that she helps you learn how to do it yourself or does she give you the answers and stuff like that.

Patient: She helps me do it myself. Sometimes she gives me the answer, but she doesn't just give me the answer, she explains why it is the answer.

Therapist: Yeah. You know, there's an old saying. See if you can figure this out. It relates to what we're talking about here. You know what proverbs are, don't you?

Patient: Yeah.

Therapist: A proverb is an old saying. This old saying goes like this. "Give a man a fish, and you've given him a meal. Teach a man *how to fish,* and you have given him a meal for life." Do you know what that means?

Patient: Uh huh.

Therapist: It means that if you've given a man a fish, you've only given him one fish, but if you teach the man how to fish, you've given him a meal for the rest of his life because he'll be able to fish by himself. Now you explain it, so I'm sure you understand.

Patient: If you just give a man a fish, he doesn't learn how to fish himself.

Therapist: Right. Very good.

Here, I suspected that the patient's mother might be doing much of the homework for him, rather than requiring him to assume most of the burden. He denied that this generally was the case and I tended to believe him. As mentioned, this mother was not as overprotective as the majority of mothers of school-phobic children. Be that as it may, I took the opportunity to present to the patient one of my favorite proverbs. It was not only relevant to David, but I have found it relevant to most patients as well. In fact, it is a good principle for the therapist to follow. Although therapy necessitates a certain amount of dependency on the therapist, the main goal should be to provide the patient with the tools to function independently.

This was one of David's last sessions. He was seen for a total of six sessions spreading over a four-week period. All of his sessions were, I believe, rich ones (the aforementioned vignettes were typical). Although he recovered more quickly than the majority of school-phobic children that I have seen, the therapeutic approach was similar.

Clinical Example -- Fred

Fred entered treatment at the age of 9½ with a school phobic problem of seven week's duration. Symptoms began on return to school following his summer vacation. Both fear and refusal elements were prominent. He provided many rationalizations for not going to school: he didn't like the teacher, the teacher didn't explain things to him, his art teacher yelled at him, he didn't like the bus driver, and he didn't like the gym teacher. All reassurances that these teachers were not as malevolent as he viewed them to be were of no avail. In addition, he was afraid that his mother would not be home on his return, but he could not specifically state where he thought she might be. Again, reassurances by her that she would indeed be at home on his return did not assuage his fear.

As mentioned, there was a significant refusal element present as well. When his parents would urge him to go to school, he would adamantly refuse. At times he would threaten to jump out of the window if they persisted. Thereupon, his mother (more than the father) would quickly relax her pressures, even though there was absolutely no evidence that Fred had any intention of carrying out his threat. (Furthermore, the window out of which he threatened to jump was either at the first- or second-story level of his home.) In addition to the suicidal threats, Fred claimed he was very depressed over the prospect of going to school and claimed suicidal preoccupations. Again, there were no concomitant evidences for significant depression.

Fred's mother was extremely overprotective, and she had practically no insight into her overprotectiveness. When he was home from school, she indulged his every whim. She had been against Fred's going to summer camp, considering him to be too young for such an experience. However, the previous summer she finally submitted to her husband's insistence that Fred go. Although he only went for two weeks, he was miserable there—steadily complaining of "homesickness." The mother believed that it had been a terrible error to have sent him, and that had he not gone he probably would not have developed his fear of going to school. Although she was probably correct here, in that the summer camp experience was a precipitating factor, she did not appreciate that the problems related to Fred's dependency upon her would have manifested themselves eventually. Fred had never visited a friend's house overnight, and his mother did not believe that he was old enough to do so. She was overconcerned about his whereabouts and feared that he might be hit by a car, drown, or suffer some other calamity.

Fred's father was a very bright engineer with a master's degree from a highly respected school of engineering. Fred's mother completed high school and then did some clerical work. She stopped working when she became pregnant with Fred's older sister and then devoted herself entirely to homemaking and child rearing. About a year prior to the onset of treatment, Fred's father left the home for a three-month period because of marital difficulties. Yet, it was clear that he was still quite dissatisfied. I suspected that this separation had played a role in producing Fred's separation anxiety. The father was clearly much more intelligent than his wife and more receptive to looking into his own role in Fred's difficulties. No meaningful therapeutic work with Fred's mother could be accomplished, but in this case I was able to rely upon the father to support the implementation of my various suggestions regarding the therapeutic program.

Because of reports in literature that imipramine (Tofranil) can be useful in the treatment of separation anxiety disorder (Gittleman-Klein and Klein, 1973; Gittleman-Klein, 1975), he was placed on 50 mg and then 75 mg every night at the time he went to sleep. There was little evidence that the medication served any purpose. I subsequently substituted diazepam (Valium) 5–10 mg p.r.n. and this appeared to be more efficacious—especially in reducing morning panic. However, I believe that the medication did not play a significant role in Fred's treatment. I believe that the enforced return to school allowed for a progressive desensitization to his separation anxieties and the therapeutic program of twice-weekly individual treatment (*after* school) were the primary factors in his improvement.

During his second week in treatment, the following interchange took place while playing the mutual storytelling game:

Patient: Once upon a time there was a mouse . . .
Therapist: A mouse?
Patient: Yeah. That lived up in the country.
Therapist: Go ahead.
Patient: And there was a mouse that lived in the city . . .

Therapist: So there's one mouse who lived in the country and one mouse who lived in the city . . . okay.

Patient: So . . . the mouse in the country had a cousin who lived in the city. . .

Therapist: Oh, they were cousins.

Patient: One day the cousin in the country invited the cousin from the city to come, to come to see the country and visit. So he went there and all they ate is seeds, grain, seeds from the ground, insects and all junk. So the city mouse said, "Come and visit the city with me because we have a lot of cheese and a lot of drinks." So they went to the city and after all the people had gone to the city, they ate cheese and cake in the city. They ate a lot of good food in the city.

Then they once found this restaurant where they served a lot of food. The country mouse ate a lot of that food and got fat. He used to eat the leftover foods that the people left on their plates. One day a black cat jumped on the table. The country mouse was so fat that he couldn't run very fast. The city mouse got away fast. But the country mouse didn't get caught either. The two of them ran to a hole and got away. The country mouse said to his cousin, "The city is terrible. I'm going back to the country. I don't like the cats you have here, and I got fat here." So he went back to the country.

The lesson of this story is: Don't go to places that are different, or you'll be sorry.

I consider the story to represent the patient's view that the world can be a dangerous place if one leaves one's home. The unfamiliar causes trouble. When the city mouse goes to the country, he is unhappy with the unappetizing diet of seeds, grain, insects, and "junk." When the country mouse goes to the city, he gets fat and is almost caught by a black cat. Accordingly, the best thing to do is stay where you are, where everything is familiar. I consider the story to reflect well Fred's view of the world as a dangerous place, and a statement of his desire to stay at home where he will be safe. With this understanding of Fred's story I told mine:

Therapist: Once upon a time there were two mice. They were cousins. One cousin lived in the country, and the other cousin lived in the city. One day the country mouse invited his city cousin to visit him. When the city cousin got there, he wasn't too happy. He didn't like the foods that they ate in the country. The ate things like seeds, grain, and insects.

He said, "This is all junk food. I don't want to eat this junk. I want to eat cheese and cake like they have in the city."

The country cousin replied, "I think you should give our food here a chance. It's not as bad as you think. It's healthy food, and it's hard to get fat on it. It's very easy to get fat on cheese and cake. I think you should give it a chance." The city mouse wasn't too happy with his country cousin's answer, but he had no choice. He really wanted to go back to the city, but he had no way to go. His parents in the city were away on vacation so he couldn't go back to his house in the city. He had to stay in the country with his country cousin until his parents returned.

After a while the city mouse began to see that his country cousin was right. He began to see that the food he was eating wasn't so bad after all. In fact, after a while he got to like it. Then he wasn't so unhappy in the country.

Then, when his parents returned from vacation, they invited the country cousin to stay with them in the city. So the two mice then returned to the city. There they began to visit a restaurant. They liked to eat the leftover foods that people left on the plates. They liked most to eat cheese and cake. The country cousin then began to get fatter. He got so fat that he was scared that he wouldn't be able to run away from cats. The city cousin told him that he didn't have to get that fat if he didn't want to. So he went on a diet and stopped eating so much cheese and cake. Then he lost weight.

One day, a big black cat came into the restaurant. As soon as the mice saw him, they ran away as fast as they could into a little hole in the corner of the restaurant. Because the two mice were thin, they had no trouble escaping from the cat. The country mouse was glad that he had listened to his cousin. He was glad that he had gone on the diet and that he wasn't too fat.

My story has two lessons. Do you know what they are?

Patient: No.

Therapist: Come on. Try to think. I think you can figure out the lessons to this story.

Patient: Uh, don't eat too much cheese and cake, or you'll get fat.

Therapist: Well, that's close to one of them. I would say that a person has control over what he does to him- or herself. If you eat too much cheese and cake, you might get fat, and if you're a mouse, you'll have trouble running away from cats. But if you do get caught by a cat, you'll have yourself to blame because you ate too much. You have the responsibility and you have the control. Now do you know what the other lesson is?

Patient: No.

Therapist: It has something to do with strange places.

Patient: You get used to them.

Therapist: Right. That's right! Strange places are not as dangerous as you might think. Because something is different doesn't mean that it's bad. Okay, do you want to watch this on television?

Patient: Yeah. I'll bring up my mother.

Therapist: Yes, we can let her watch this. However, I told you before that we're not going to let her stay here with us very much. I know you didn't want to let her out before, but it's against the rules of your treatment for her to be with you all the time.

It is obvious what I have done in my responding story. I have addressed myself to the pathological elements in the patient's story and have introduced what I consider to be healthier modes of resolution. I attempted to entrench the notion that gaining knowledge and competence enhances one's capacity to adjust in the world. As mentioned, this is the most important route to the alleviation of symptoms. In Fred's case, I then applied this principle to adjusting in strange places, hoping to reduce thereby his separation anxiety. Although the patient was coughing somewhat nervously at certain points in my story, he certainly stuck with it until the end. With a little help he was able to understand the story's basic messages.

Fred's treatment lasted about six months. About three months after Fred began therapy his father once again left the home. I considered the earlier separation between the parents to have been one of the precipitating factors in Fred's separation anxiety disorder. However, he did not suffer an exacerbation of his symptoms. He gradually returned to the classroom and became progressively tolerant of spending a full day there. I believe that the transitional phase in the resource room was useful for Fred, as it is for many children with school phobias. Although his mother never gained much insight into what was going on, she was able to tolerate more the separation from Fred. In addition, unlike the parent's previous separation, in this separation Fred spent more time with his father and they engaged in more age-appropriate activities than they had been involved in during the previous separation. Some time was spent in helping Fred deal more appropriately with his anger, so that he would not have to handle it by projection and reaction formation. As is often the case in the treatment of children with separation anxiety disorder, the therapeutic improvement, I believe, was less related to dealing with the anger problems than the desensitization to the phobic situation and progressive maturation in all areas of functioning.

Clinical Example -- Bonnie

Bonnie, a 10-year-old fourth grade girl, entered therapy with a severe school phobia of three weeks' duration. The symptom started a few days after the assassination of President Kennedy, at a time when her maternal grandmother was on the verge of dying of cancer. Upon arising in the morning she would complain of headache, nausea, vomiting, and palpitations. As she approached school, she became increasingly panicky, clung to her mother ever more tenaciously, and would refuse to part from her to enter school. She claimed to be frightened of her teacher who was in reality a somewhat mild-mannered woman whom she had never feared before.

There was no past history of school fears (with the exception of fear of separating from her mother during the first two weeks of the first grade). From the age of five she had frequently reacted with exaggerated anxiety to minor physical illnesses, was preoccupied with "scary ghosts," was fearful of going to friends' homes, exhibited occasional facial tics, and was generally timid about playing rough games or exposing herself to even slightly dangerous situations such as riding her bicycle on the street.

The patient's mother was an extremely materialistic woman whose main pleasures were exhibiting her fine home and showing off her expensive clothing. She was not a particularly maternal woman and left the primary care of her two children to housekeepers. Bonnie's father was a successful lawyer. Although he complained of his wife's extravagance, he definitely enjoyed her displays of his wealth. He was severely claustrophobic in elevators, subways, and small rooms when the doors were closed. In addition, he was very involved with occult phenomena, communication with the dead, and various forms of extrasensory perception.

During the first few minutes of each session I discussed with the patient and her mother various problems that arose in the household, both the school problem and others. Like most mothers of school phobics, Bonnie's mother had difficulty following through with my suggestions. Besides the realistic discomforts treatment caused her to suffer, her own ambivalence contributed to her inability to follow through completely. However, the therapist cannot wait to analyze the mother's ambivalence "away." She too must learn to exert some conscious control, push through her own anxieties (just as her child is doing), and get the child to school. In spite of all the brouhaha at home and school, Bonnie (like most school phobics) settled down to a conventional session in my office. We spent some time playing the storytelling game and the rest of the session was spent in the traditional manner working both with the patient and her parents. Although the focus here is on the storytelling sequences, other relevant aspects of Bonnie's treatment are described.

Bonnie's first story in treatment was about a kitten who was singled out for rejection by the mother cat and sold to another family which she subsequently left because of cruel treatment. The kitten then suffered a series of further harrowing experiences in catland and dogland before Bonnie woke from the nightmare.

During her second week of treatment, Bonnie told this story:

Once upon a time there were three boys and three girls, and the boys wanted to spy on the girls. So they put a tape recorder in the room where the girls were and a walkie-talkie in there so that they could hear them and tape what they say.

So the girls found out about this and so they decided that they should do a trick on the boys, so they said into the walkie-talkie and the tape recorder that they were going to spy on the boys. So the boys said, "Let's tell on the girls that they are going to spy on us." So they went in and told.

Therapist: Who did they tell?

Patient: Their mother. And so they went in and told their mother.

Therapist: Were all of these children brothers and sisters?

Patient: Yes. And so then the mother called the girls into the house and asked if they were going to spy on the boys, and they said, "No." And so then the girls asked one of the boys how they knew that they were planning to spy. So then the boys had to tell that they were spying on them. So that's the end.

Therapist: What was the moral of that story?

Patient: That you shouldn't tattle on something that you did yourself.

Therapist: Don't tattle on someone if you do the same thing yourself.

Patient: Yes

Therapist: I see. Thank you very much, Bonnie.

The story is typical of an early resistance story. The brothers represent the therapist and the girls symbolize the patient. The tape recorder and walkie-talkie which are used for spying are the therapist's devices for finding out things Bonnie does not wish to disclose. The girls foil the boys' plot, preventing further use of the bugging devices. In this way the patient satisfies her wish for privacy and protects herself from the dangers of revealing herself to me. Accordingly I told this story:

> Once upon a time there were three boys and three girls and one of these girls was upset about something and she was seeing a psychiatrist. And the psychiatrist once brought in the whole family and he said, "I'd like to get information about this girl that will help me treat her." And the girl said, "Uh, uh, uh. I don't want you to get information from my family. I don't want to let them know what's going on inside my mind." And the psychiatrist then said, "Well, this is the best way that I could help you. If I learn what is going on in your mind then I can help you with your problems. If I don't, then I can't." And the girl said, "Well, I'm a little hesitant to do that."
>
> The psychiatrist said, "How about putting a walkie-talkie or a tape recorder in your room so that the things you do or say will be heard and then we can listen to the tapes and learn about your problems?"
>
> Well, she was hesitant to do it. In fact, she said no. Then one of her sisters had similar problems, but this sister agreed that it might be helpful if she let them put the walkie-talkie and the tape recorder in her room. And much to her amazement, she found out that when she listened to it and when she discussed it with the doctor, she learned a lot about her troubles that she hadn't known before. And then the other sister seeing this said, "Well, all right. Try it on me too." And then they tried it on her and then both sisters got better.
>
> The lesson of this story is that sometimes it may be frightening to reveal things about yourself to a psychiatrist, but when you do, you'll find out that it helps you very much with your problems. The end.

My story needs no interpretation. Bonnie listened with interest. Three days later, she told this story:

> Once upon a time there was this baby eagle and he lived on this nest high on top of a mountain with his brother, and his sisters and his mother and father.
>
> One day he asked his mother if he could try to fly. And his mother said, "No, you're not old enough yet." But he still wanted to fly.

So then one day when his mother was out he crawled out from his nest and tried to fly. He couldn't fly and he fell, but he kept on falling and falling. Finally, his mother saw him falling and she ran to him and caught him. And then she put him back in the nest and he never tried to fly again. And that's the end.

The moral of the story is that you shouldn't try things that you are not suppose to.

The baby eagle is Bonnie whose overprotective mother tries to discourage her from flying, that is, from acting like an adult and going out alone into the world. Instead she would have her remain longer in the nest—an infantile state of dependence. The metaphor is accurate. Bonnie's mother was quite fearful of the patient's exposing herself to the slightest dangers (bike-riding in the street, swimming in deep water, walking long distances, etc.).

When Bonnie does disobey her mother and attempts to assume some independence, the results are catastrophic. Mother's prophecy is fulfilled. The patient cannot get along without her, and she never flies again. She resigns herself, in other words, to a life in the womb.

The story reveals one of the important elements in Bonnie's fear of going to school. School is a place which teaches her to fly, that is, to be independent of mother. Although her mother ostensibly wanted her to go to school, there was another part of her that would keep the patient dependent and infantile. Bonnie's symptom was, in part, a compliance with her mother's unconscious wish that Bonnie never grow up. Accordingly, I told this story:

Once upon a time there was a baby eagle and he was in a nest with his brothers and sisters and mother and father. And he asked his mother if he could fly. His mother said, "No, you're too young. There are lots of dangerous things out in the world and you'd better stay in your nest."

So the next week he said, "Could I fly now, Momma?" And the mother said, "No, I'm very sorry. You are not old enough. It's dangerous out there. You listen to what I said."

Well, week in and week out he asked his mother and she said, "No, I want you to stay in the nest and stay around here."

Well, he looked over at the other trees and he saw other little eagles who were born around the same time he was and were just as old as he. They were starting to fly. And he said to the mother, "The other eagles are flying." And she said, "That's all right. Their mothers don't care for them the way that I care for you and I want you to stay around the nest, stay around the house."

Well, he listened to his mother and he watched the other eagles flying all around, getting bigger and bigger, and he started getting angrier and angrier because he was missing out on all the fun. The eagles were playing games and things in the air and flying about and going down into the water and up into the air and swinging all around. And he felt very jealous of them and he felt very angry at his mother until he finally said, "The heck with her."

One day he flew out of the nest and joined the other eagles and they said, "Oh, we're glad to see you. We were wondering when you were going to grow up and stop being a little baby and staying home. We are happy you are around."

Well, anyway, he did that and his mother got kind of angry at him, but he said, "You can't stop me. You can't stop me from growing up and being a big eagle like everyone else." Then the mother had no choice but to let him go, and although she was the kind of mother who tried to keep her children infants so that they would always be with her and she wouldn't be lonely, she realized that there was nothing she could do about it.

The lesson of my story is that if your mother is the kind of person who wants to keep you in the house, try not to listen to her.

Patient: Right!

Therapist: Go out and have fun. If you are the kind that stays in the house all the time you're going to miss out on a lot of good things and a lot of good times. The end.

My story elaborates on the pleasures of independence as part of my approach to helping Bonnie break the umbilical cord: "The eagles were playing games and things in the air and flying about and going down into the water and up into the air and swinging all around." In addition, I confronted her with the unpleasant fact that being tied to mother's apron strings subjects one to a certain amount of criticism from one's peers: "We were wondering when you were going to grow up and stop being a little baby and staying home." I put Bonnie in touch with some of the anger she must harbor within her for allowing herself to be squelched by her mother: "he started getting angrier and angrier because he was missing out on all the fun." I communicated the message that if she is to take steps toward independence, she will invoke her mother's anger but that this is not so dangerous as she anticipates. In fact, mother is somewhat impotent to stop her in many areas: "Then the mother had no choice but to let him go ... she realized that there was nothing she could do about it." Bonnie's single word response to my story—"Right!"— was stated with such enthusiasm that there was no question that my story had "reached" her.

Following my story, I asked the patient if her mother let her do the things other children do. She complained bitterly: "My mother and father don't let me ride my bike in the street the way other kids my age do. She won't let me swim in the deep end of the pool and I'm a good swimmer. I couldn't cross the street alone in front of my house until I was eight. I couldn't go to school alone until I was eight, and all the other kids in my class were going alone. She wouldn't let me play under the bridge over the brook where all the other kids used to play."

The mother was then brought in. She described how the maternal grandmother, who lived in the home until Bonnie was eight, was constantly concerned for the welfare of everyone in the family. If Bonnie were five minutes late, the grandmother expressed fears that she had been killed. She would wait up until Bonnie's parents came home, regardless of the hour, stating: "I can't go to sleep until they're home. I keep worrying that something will happen to them." In short, Bonnie had been programmed, from the beginning of her life, to see the world as a dangerous place. Death lurked everywhere; the only safe place was home with mother. Considering her family's continual state of fear, it was surprising that she wasn't more phobic than she was.

The therapist must decide how much he can expect a child to accomplish on his or her own and how much assistance the patient will need. Helping the child too much may foster pathological dependency; expecting the child to handle a task that is beyond his or her capabilities may be overwhelming and intensify the child's difficulties. In this case, I felt that Bonnie would need some assistance, and so I arranged for an interview with Bonnie and her parents. We focused on their irrational fears. They were able to see some of them as inappropriate and subsequently alter them; others they could not. For example, they were willing to give her greater freedom in the neighborhood and in the swimming pool. However, the mother could do nothing about her airplane phobia, and the father could not be expected to cease his life-long claustrophobic reactions. Both parents agreed that their fears were irrational, but they could not help themselves. This was an important admission, and I emphasized it to Bonnie during the meeting. When parents exhibit behavior that they recognize as inappropriate but which they cannot control, it can be helpful to the child for such parents to define to the child the exact area of pathology and state directly and unequivocally to the child that, although they cannot help themselves, they recognize the illogicality of their thinking and feelings. In this way there is less likelihood that the distorted notions will be transmitted to the child. If they have already been revealed as described, then clarification of their irrationality to the child can be helpful. Some parents are hesitant to reveal their defects because of the fear that their children will lose respect for them. The child is usually aware, at some level, of the parents' inadequacies and respects them less if they hide them than if they are mature enough to openly admit them. One of the therapist's goals in treatment is to help children gain a clearer view of their parents; their assets and their liabilities; their strengths and their weaknesses. Such clarification can only be salutary. In Bonnie's case it helped her remove some of the irrational dictates that she had learned from her parents and that were contributing to her fears.

A number of such family interviews were held during the first few months of treatment in order to ensure that Bonnie view her parents more accurately. In addition, the parents were advised to reiterate the new insights at home.

During her fourth week in treatment, Bonnie told this story:

> Once upon a time there were these three cats and they lived alone all by themselves. There was this new cat who moved near them. They sort of liked her but she didn't act like she liked them or anything. They wanted to make friends with her but they were afraid to ask her because they thought she might not like them or anything.
>
> So one day they were building this house—the first three cats were building this clubhouse. And so they were almost done when they saw this other cat toss this ball—roll it with its feet, you know. And so it ruined their clubhouse and then they knew that that cat really didn't like them and they thought she did it on purpose.

Therapist: Wait a minute. That fourth cat threw a ball towards the others?

Patient: Yes. He threw a ball towards the clubhouse and it fell down. And so one day she came over—

Therapist: What did they think about her throwing the ball? How did they interpret that?

Patient: Then they really knew that she didn't like them, and they didn't think that they wanted to play with her. And so they just forgot about her and, you know, and stayed away from her for all the wrong purpose and all.

And so then the next day the other cat—the one they didn't want to play with—came over and she said that she would like to play with them. No, that she was sorry about ruining the clubhouse and that it was an accident. So then they knew that she really did like them. And so then they were sort of glad that she wrecked the clubhouse because then they wouldn't have found out that she really liked them. And then they all played together.

The lesson of the story is sometimes you find out that you like somebody when you think you don't.

Therapist: Was this fourth cat a male or a female cat?

Patient: A female cat. They were all girls.

In one part of the story, the fourth cat is referred to as male: "He threw a ball towards the clubhouse and it fell down." Elsewhere, the fourth cat is referred to as "she" and is identified as female when I specifically asked its sex at the end. Considering the fourth cat male provides, in my opinion, the most meaningful interpretation. I am the fourth cat and the other three represent Bonnie and her parents. I'm the new "cat" who moves into the neighborhood. The three cats are hesitant about the newcomer: "They thought she might not like them." The clubhouse is the wall the patient builds to protect herself from my intrusions into her privacy. I penetrate her defenses —I ruin their clubhouse by rolling a ball against it. Their first response to this was to stay away from the fourth cat—no good can come from Bonnie's associating herself with me. I then explain to them that I meant no harm and that I really want to be her friend, and she accepts this. In essence Bonnie is telling me that she understands that I may cause her some pain in removing her protective shell, but that she realizes that my motives are basically benevolent. The moral epitomizes her feelings: "Sometimes you find out that you like somebody when you think you don't."

The story reveals a diminution of Bonnie's resistances and reflects increasing trust of me—the two, perforce, go together. In response, I told this story:

Once upon a time there were three cats. Now these three cats lived alone and one day a fourth cat moved into the neighborhood. And this cat wanted to be friendly with the three cats but they were kind of suspicious at first and they didn't know whether the fourth cat was really to be trusted or not.

And then one day this fourth cat rolled a ball over, and the fourth cat rolled the ball over as a sign of friendship. He wanted to be friends but they didn't interpret it right. They thought it wasn't friendship, that this cat was trying to hurt them.

Well, the next day the cat came over and told them that he wanted to be friends—mine is a boy cat—they were still a little distrustful, but they said, "Okay, we'll give him a chance." Now then this cat, as part of being friends, started to ask them a lot of questions about themselves. First they thought, "This is kind of personal." And they said to him, "Those are personal questions that you are asking." He said, "Isn't that part of being friends? When you are friendly with someone you are kind of personal and tell them things about yourself." Well, they thought about that and they realized that that was right. In real close friendships, you tell a lot of personal things. So they began to realize that the fourth cat really wanted to be their friend because he spoke about a number of personal things. And so then they started to talk about personal things and they felt much closer to him and they were very happy because then they could go to him with problems and troubles and he would try to help them with their problems and troubles when they told him personal things. Sometimes he told them personal things about himself and asked their advice.

And the lesson of that story is that in a good friendship you can tell the other person personal things because then you can help one another. The end.

Whereas in her story my intrusion—breaking down the clubhouse—was initially seen as painful and traumatic, in mine a less distorted view is presented. What she sees as an encroachment upon her privacy is really my way of demonstrating my interest and affection. Mutual revelation of intimacies is the cornerstone of friendship. In my story, then, I emphasized those elements in her story that reflected increasing trust and diminishing resistance in order to further reinforce and entrench these newly formed attitudes.

Less than a month later (near the end of her second month of treatment), Bonnie told this story:

Once there were two monkeys, a boy and a girl. They were brother and sister and their father told them: "Go out in the jungle and pick some bananas." So they went out and they looked all over the place, but they couldn't find banana trees. Then they went into a nearby jungle and they saw big palm trees and so on the palm trees they looked up there wasn't bananas on the palm trees, but there were coconuts. "Let's explain to our father that we couldn't find any bananas and I'm sure he won't mind having coconuts." But they didn't know that monkeys hate coconuts because they never tried them

So they brought the coconuts home to their father and the father got real real mad and he said, "You know, monkeys hate coconuts. How dare you come back without bringing back bananas?" They said, "We couldn't find any." He said, "Well, that's no excuse for bringing back coconuts." So the little girl said, "How come you don't like coconuts? How come monkeys don't like coconuts?" The father said "Well they never have." And they said, "Why?" And the father said, "Well, monkeys are used to eating bananas." And so the boy said, "Well, why don't you try it and see?" The father said, "No, that's ridiculous. No monkeys have ever liked bananas—I mean coconuts." The little boy said, "Yes, but you never tried it and none of your parents did. So maybe they do like it." The father said, "Well, only to prove to you, I'll take bananas all day."

Therapist: Coconuts.

Patient: Coconuts. "Only to prove to you that monkeys hate coconuts, I'll do it and also you two will taste it." So first the children taste it and they say, "It's not bad. It's pretty good." Then the father says. "Oh, you're just lying so that will be an excuse for me liking it." So then the father tried them and then he waited a little bit and then he said, "Hey, they are good."

Then he went all over the jungle to his monkey friends and told them there aren't many bananas now, but to try coconuts. So they all did and then the monkeys all liked coconuts afterwards.

Therapist: And the moral?

Patient: You don't know whether you'll like something unless you try it.

Therapist: Okay. Very good.

The story reveals Bonnie's willingness to try new things; to incorporate ideas which are alien to her parents; and even to attempt to change those of her parents' deep-seated notions that she considers irrational. The new ideas, of course, are the altered attitudes about the world which are replacing distortions derived from her parents. At the time of the telling of this story, definite clinical improvement was noted. Bonnie was less fearful of going to school but still required a fair amount of coaxing. She was, however, remaining in the classroom throughout the day, about half the time— a marked improvement.

In response, I told this story:

Once upon a time there were two monkeys, a brother and a sister and they lived on the edge of the jungle with their father. Now this father was a very funny old man. He had some strange ideas. He used to say, "Now children don't go into the jungle. It's very dangerous in the jungle. All kinds of dangerous things can happen to you. Be very careful not to eat the coconuts. Don't eat the bananas or else you might get sick. Be very careful. Stay right around the house. Stay right around our hut— our monkey hut."

Well, these kids grew up believing that all this was so. They would see other monkeys go into the jungle and the other monkeys seemed to be all right, but these kids somehow still kept on believing that these things were dangerous. They would see a monkey coming out eating bananas and they would say, "Oh, he's eating bananas. He's going to get sick." They'd see another monkey eating coconuts and they'd say, "Ooh, he's eating coconuts. He's going to get sick. Ooh, he's playing in the jungle. Terrible things are going to happen to him." But they never saw any terrible thing happen. Nobody got sick from bananas. Nobody got sick from coconuts and nobody got hurt in the jungle.

So one day some kid came over to them and said, "Why don't you come on. We'll play in the jungle." They said, "Ooh, no. It's dangerous in the jungle." He replied, "Where did you get that idea?" He said, "My father told me." The kid said, "That's absurd. There's nothing to be frightened of in the jungle. Sure once in a while something may happen that's a little dangerous, but that is very seldom." Anyway, that got the monkeys thinking and they gradually began to realize that maybe their father wasn't right.

So one day they very carefully, very hesitantly stepped into the jungle and although they were scared at first, they gradually came to realize that the jungle wasn't a frightening thing or a frightening place. One day they even got the guts to try and taste a coconut. They did it and they found out that it was really pretty good and the same thing with a banana. So it ended up with their playing in the jungle and eating coconuts and bananas. At first their father was kind of upset, but then they said, "Look, we're big enough to make these decisions on our own. If you don't want to go into the jungle that's your problem. You can do what you want, but we're going into the jungle. We're going to have a good time."

Do you know what the moral of that story is?

Patient: I don't know.

Therapist: Can you try to figure it out?

Patient: That sometimes things aren't really as dangerous as people say they are.

Therapist: Right! And that's the moral of that story. The end. What did you think of that story?

Patient: It was good.

My story is also on the theme of changing parental precepts. I advised Bonnie to judge the world on the basis of her own observations and not blindly accept her parents' notions. She is encouraged to consider new and different ways of doing things and to have living experiences that will better enable her to evaluate the ideas that she has indiscriminately incorporated from her parents. She is urged to push through the inevitable anxieties associated with exposure to such new experiences. Lastly, Bonnie is advised to stand up and resist her father should he interfere with her in these pursuits: "Look, we're big enough to make these decisions on our own. If you don't want to go into the jungle that's your problem. You can do what you want, but we're going into the jungle. We're going to have a good time." The patient accurately provided a moral, "Sometimes things aren't really as dangerous as people say they are," and her final comment that my story was a "good" one was said with conviction and pleasure.

Seven weeks later, during the middle of her fourth month of treatment, Bonnie told this story:

Once upon a time there were two kids. They were girls. They decided they wanted to go into a tunnel. One of the girls was very scared. She said, "I don't want to go. We might get trapped. It might rain and water will gush in." The second girl was scared too and she said, "You're right."

Then their brother said that there was nothing to worry about. He went in and they followed him and everything was okay. There was nothing to fear. Then the brother said, "There are rats in here." The girls knew he was only kidding and they laughed.

The moral of that story is: sometimes if you try something it might turn out okay. Things are safer than it looks.

The story represents another attempt to desensitize herself to situations which she has come to associate with danger. Near Bonnie's home was a brook which flowed under a bridge. Although many of the neighborhood children played there, prior to therapy, Bonnie's mother had prohibited her from joining them. The tunnel in the patient's story, where water might gush in, symbolizes, I believe, the once forbidden brook under the bridge. She accustoms herself to this dangerous place which represents all perilous places and, in addition, uses counterphobic mechanisms to assuage her anxiety: the girls laugh when their brother tells them there are rats in the tunnel.

Although the story suggests further improvment, it was told during her summer vacation from school. Only the future could determine how much of the changes exhibited in therapy would carry over into the classroom.

In response, I told this story:

> Once upon a time there was an amusement park. It was a playland, but you had to crawl through a long tunnel in order to get there. The amusement park was at the end of the tunnel. There were three kids, two girls and a boy, who wanted to get to the amusement park, but they were first fearful of going through the tunnel. The girls especially were scared of getting scratched and rubbed along the sides of the tunnel. The boy, although he was scared too, said that there are a lot of things in life that you have to go to trouble for if you are to enjoy them. So they started crawling through the tunnel. They got hurt a little, a few scratches and a few bruises, but they finally got to the playland and they were happy that they had gone to all the trouble.
>
> Do you know what the moral of this story is?
>
> *Patient:* Sometimes if you go through a lot of trouble it's worth it.
> *Therapist:* Yes. That's the moral of this story. There are many times in life when you have to suffer minor inconveniences in order to get the rewards at the end.

Whereas in Bonnie's story there are no dangers, in mine there are some to correspond with the way life really is. They are, however, not so terrible as her parents would have her believe. If she wishes to pursue pleasurable goals in life (the amusement park) she will have to expose herself to certain minor traumata (the scratches and bruises in my story). I make the point that most are willing to suffer these inconveniences for the pleasures they ultimately attain.

During her fifth month of treatment Bonnie returned to school after her summer vacation. There was anxiety, nausea, and balking but far less than she had had prior to the summer.

During her sixth month of treatment, after she had been back in school about a month, she became increasingly phobic. I could not attribute the exacerbation to any specific event or experience at school or home, and considered it to be a manifestation of the common phenomenon in treatment that with advances there comes anxiety which, in turn, is reduced by regression. At this time, Bonnie told this story:

> Once there were these kids and they wanted to watch a certain TV show. So they turned on the TV set and they found out that it was too early and it wasn't time for it. So they turned the TV off and went and played and rode their bicycles and did other things. So then one kid said, "Maybe it's time to go back in and watch the show. Maybe it's on now." Nobody else listened to him. They were having fun playing and doing other things. So the other kid just stayed out too. So finally they all got tired and they went inside and said, "Maybe it's on by now." So they turned the TV set on and they found out that they had missed the show. Because they didn't pay attention or think about what they were doing, they missed what they wanted to see—the show they wanted to watch.
>
> *Therapist:* And the lesson of that story?
> *Patient:* Pay attention and watch the time on whatever it is that you're doing if there's something you want to see because you might miss it if you don't pay attention.
> *Therapist:* Thank you very much. Now it's time for me to tell my story.

This is a typical example of a resistance story. The picture on the television screen is what Bonnie would see in treatment if she looked into herself. It is the projection of unconscious processes. She is ambivalent about such inquiry at this time and the story reflects it. Various rationalizations are utilized to justify her not looking at herself, and the story ends with successful avoidance. With this interpretation in mind, I told this story:

> Once upon a time there were some children who said they wanted to watch a TV show. Now this was a show—it was one of these family shows— and it told about things that happened between parents and children and it was a kind of serious family show. These kids had kind of mixed feelings about watching this show because they knew deep down that some of the things that would be happening on this show might be a little upsetting to them. But they said, "Let's watch the show." First they turned on the television set and it was too early. So

they went outside and they started to play. Then one of them said, "Shall we go back and see if the show is on yet." The others didn't listen. They just wanted to play. So finally after they played a long time they decided to go in, but by that time it was too late and the show had been over. But they had a kind of sigh of relief that it was over. They were also a little sad that they had missed it, because although it would have been a little upsetting, they might have learned some things from this family show that might have been helpful to them. All things considered, they ended up sorry that they had missed it.

The moral of that story is—what's the moral of that story?
Patient: I don't know.
Therapist: The moral of that story is that if you do look at something that may be a little upsetting that you may learn something even though it may be a little upsetting. Don't run away from things just because they're a little upsetting. If you do you may miss out on some good things.

In my story I tried to create some incentive for Bonnie to look into herself once again because she might then learn things about herself which might be helpful to her. Another tack I often take with such stories utilizing television and movies is to have the children tolerate the anxieties they have about viewing the scary show. They then find that it not only wasn't as bad as they had anticipated, but that they learned some interesting things as well.

A week after this interchange, Bonnie's grandmother died. Fortunately, there was no intensification of her symptoms. During the subsequent weeks there was further improvement.

In the middle of her seventh month of therapy, Bonnie told this story:

Once there were these deers and they lived in the forest with a lot of other little animals. They didn't have very much fun in the winter because it got cold and it was hard to find food some of the days. But they had fun playing in the snow and all. Then in the summer they had fun too, but the hunters always came hunting sometimes in the summer. So they really didn't want to go out and play around too much in the summer.

So one time there were two little deers and they were pretty afraid of the hunter, so they always stayed inside and watched TV and played games. They didn't go outside and run around much. Everyone was telling them—all the other little deers, and rabbits and birds and chipmunks and all—"The hunters don't come around too much. Why don't you come out and play a little bit?" They said, "No, if he comes we'll be in a lot of trouble." So their parents thought it was a better idea for them to stay inside too.

So one day their grandfather came over and he said to them, "Why don't you come for a walk with me in the woods?" They said, "No, the hunters will get us." He said, "Of course not. I've been going walking around in the forest for years and I haven't gotten hurt by a hunter. Anyway, we're too fast for the hunters to catch us." So at first they were kind of scared to go out, but then, you know, the grandfather kept telling them how simple it was to get away from the hunters and they went outside. They went outside and they played around and the parents knew that they had gone out with the grandfather. They were very angry and they were afraid that they might get hurt by the hunters. So then they all came in very excited and the little deer said, "Boy, we sure had a lot of fun." The mother said, "You mean no hunters came after you?" He only said, "Oh, sure a lot of hunters came after us. The most fun was running away from them and playing games so they couldn't catch us. Grandpa showed us how." So the parents weren't afraid and the little deers weren't afraid to go out in the woods anymore.

Therapist: The lesson of that story?

Patient: That things can be less dangerous sometimes if you—you shouldn't be too afraid if things are going to be very dangerous 'cause sometimes they are not dangerous and if you try, you might not get hurt or anything.

Therapist: Excellent story. Excellent story. Okay. I have a question. How is it that the hunters came in the summertime and not in the wintertime?

Patient: 'Cause in the wintertime it was too cold and in the summertime it was easier to find the animals because they were all out.

Therapist: And in the wintertime?

Patient: In the wintertime they were usually inside because of the cold.

Therapist: I see. Thank you very much. That was an excellent story and now it's time for me to tell my story.

The story reflects the clinical improvement Bonnie had enjoyed since the last sequence presented. She once again exposes herself to the phobic situation and finds that her fears were unfounded. In addition, counterphobic phenomena are present: tempting the hunters and then eluding them is fun. Like the boy who whistles as he walks through the cemetery at night, making believe she isn't scared helps in the desensitization process. The story also reveals her appreciation of her parent's role in her symptoms and her overt refutation of their irrational dictates.

In response, I told this story:

Once upon a time there were these two deer and they lived in the forest with the other little animals. These two deer had parents who were always seeing frightening things happening in the forest and they would exaggerate every little danger and make it a big thing. For instance, when the two deer went out in the winter their mother would say, "Don't catch a cold. Be careful. You're out in the cold. Don't catch a cold." The mother would worry, "Oh, there's so little food out there in the wintertime. Maybe they'll starve." She was constantly worried that they'd sink into the snow or get hurt or suffocate —things like that. So the mother was constantly worried. In the summer she would worry about the hunters. Sure an occasional hunter would go through, but this mother was constantly worried that these little deer would be killed by hunters. Well, as a result of that, these deer hardly went out. They didn't go out in the wintertime because their mother was afraid of colds, starvation, suffocation. They didn't go out in the summertime because the mother was afraid of death by being shot.

Anyway, one day the grandfather came and he said, "Why aren't you kids out playing? The little deer said, "Oh, there are dangerous things out there in the world." He said, "What kind of dangerous things?" The little girls—they were girl deer—said, "Well, first of all, in the wintertime it's very cold and we can catch cold." He said, "Oh, fiddlesticks. What kind of junk is that? You aren't going to get colds that way. Colds are caused by germs. Just because you feel a little bit cold outside doesn't mean you'll catch a cold. That's a disease. All the kids are out there on their sleds, throwing snowballs, having a lot of fun. There's no reason why you kids shouldn't be out there playing. Your parents don't know what they're talking about." Then they said, "Also, there's not too much food out there." He said, "So what will happen? You're not going to starve. You're just going out for a little while. Nothing is going to happen. You get plenty of food here at home where you live in this cave and nothing is going to happen to you." Then they said, "What about sinking into the snow and suffocating?" He said, "That's a lot of bunk too. The snow isn't that deep out there. I've never heard of a deer suffocating in the snow." Anyway, he just pooh-poohed all these fears that their parents had. Then they said, "Well, what about in the summertime? You know there are hunters out there in the summer." "Yeah," he said, "there's a hunter once in a while, but you know how to run pretty fast. There's no reason to be so afraid of all these things. Your parents have some strange ideas about the dangers of the world."

Anyway, they talked more to the parents and the parents kind of admitted that they knew that their fears weren't really realistic. They really didn't believe it too much, but they couldn't help being frightened.

So the little deer said, "Let's try it." So they went out with their grandfather both in the summertime and in the wintertime. Sure they occasionally met a hunter, but, number one, this hunter, first of all, wasn't going around shooting baby deer, and number two, they were pretty sensitive and when they would smell a hunter from a distance, before the hunter would even see them, they would get out of the way. Sure there was a rare, occasional danger, but certainly nothing like the parents had described. So these two deer gradually realized that their parents' ideas of the world were not very true, that their parents had some exaggerated fears about the world, and when they went out and saw that it wasn't that way, they felt much better about things. They had much more fun, played with other kids, began to enjoy themselves much more, and then grew up to be happy, healthy deer.

The lesson of that story is—do you know what the lesson is?

Patient: No.

Therapist: The lesson of that story is: Not all the things that your parents teach you about the dangers in the world are necessarily true. You have to look for yourself and see if it is true or not. The end. What do you think about that story?

Patient: It was a good story.

Therapist: What was the part about it you liked?

Patient: I liked it all. I don't think I liked any part better than I liked the whole part.

Therapist: I think yours was an excellent story too. I think these are very good stories. Do you think these stories have anything to do with your situation in school?

Patient: No, not in school.

Therapist: Nothing at all?

Patient: No.

Therapist: Hhmmm. I think it has a little bit to do with it in this regard. You think that there are terribly dangerous things happening in school which aren't happening.

Patient: The mother deer sounds like my maid.

Therapist: The mother?

Patient: Last winter—

Therapist: Which maid? What was her name?

Patient: Hilda. And she was so afraid I didn't have five sweaters on and

I had these big boots and sometimes, you know, she wanted me to wear kneesocks. I just wore summer socks because I had big furry boots. I could be just walking out the door with my sled and she'd have to check my socks to see if they were kneesocks.

Therapist: Well, what did your mother and father do about this?

Patient: My mother went along with her pretty much.

Therapist: What do you think about that?

Patient: I think that's a little stupid.

Therapist: I think so too.

Patient: I was wearing—I wore like snowpants with pants under them and a shirt, a ski windbreaker, a pullover sweater, and they still don't think I'm warm enough.

Therapist: They have these exaggerated fears that I was talking about. Some terrible thing will happen to you. You've got to protect yourself at all times from colds or terrible dangers in the world. Huh?

Patient: Hhmmm.

Therapist: That's one of your family's problems, you know.

Patient: They used to be afraid that I'd drown.

Therapist: When was that?

Patient: When we'd go to the hotel. When we went to a hotel when I was in third grade or fourth grade or second grade and I knew how to swim pretty well for a long time, but they have ropes sometimes that divide the real shallow end from the deep end. I could swim in the deeper end, but in first grade I didn't pass my deep-water test at Town and Country Day Camp, and so by the time I was in third grade I wanted to go past the ropes in any swimming pool. "Well, you didn't pass the deep water test. You can't go swimming until you pass your deep water test, and I wasn't even going to day camp then."

Therapist: Hhmmm. So your parents are always frightened that something is going to happen to you? Huh?

Patient: Yes.

Therapist: And I think that's what happens to you in school. When you're in school you're kind of locked into a place which is separate from your home, and I think you think that terrible things can happen to you there. What do you think of that?

Patient: I don't know.

Therapist: You've been exposed to so much talk that things are dangerous that you've come to believe it yourself. You've come to believe that the world is a more dangerous place than it is. What do you think of that?

Patient: I think that's right. My father was always afraid to go in elevators and he used to tell me how everytime he got stuck in elevators. So up until fourth grade I was afraid to go on elevators.

Therapist: Well, how did you decide to change?

Patient: Well, when we go to hotels, I make friends usually and we play games, like in the elevators, if there isn't any operator in it. We, well, let's take when Alice and I went down to Florida over the weekend. There's four different hotels but they have one big lobby. There's a lot of different elevators and there's this boy here who was the son of a friend of my father's, and we got into this screwy elevator that was different from our elevator, I mean it was in a different section, in a different building from ours, and something was screwy because it always kept stopping at eight. Alice ran out of the elevator when it opened at eight. She wasn't sure she wanted to get in it, and I stayed in and then I pushed the button and then I ran out. But the boy Ralph, he didn't run too, so we got the next elevator and we kept on pushing all the elevator buttons, but we couldn't find him until about a half-hour later. He was coming down in one of the elevators. It was very funny.

Therapist: That's how you stopped being afraid of elevators?

Patient: Oh, well, no. I have ridden in elevators before then, but that's what I do with my friends if we're at a hotel or something.

Therapist: Hhmmm. Well, I think your fear of going to school has something to do with all these other things you've been told about—how dangerous things are in the world. What do you think?

Patient: I don't know.

Therapist: Do you think there might be something to what I just said?

Patient: Uh huh.

Therapist: Have you come to realize that many of the things that your parents are afraid of are really nonsense?

Patient: Yeah.

Therapist: That your father's fear of elevators—your father's afraid sometimes in restaurants and theaters and things like that—all kinds of closed places, you know.

Patient: Yeah.

Therapist: Don't you think that's kind of foolish when you see him so frightened?

Patient: Yes, and when I went to The Roosevelt School, the school was right down the road from me, but you just had to cross the street, and all my other friends would be going alone, but I had to have my little maid take me across the street.

Therapist: Why was that?

Patient: 'Cause my parents were afraid for me to cross the street. So finally the last two weeks of second grade or something I was allowed to cross the street by myself. The maid would walk down to the school and watch me cross the street by myself and then I was very big.

Therapist: So you thought a lot of their concern was kind of silly. Huh?

Patient: Uh huh.

Therapist: But, you know, I think you are still afraid of one big thing. From all this stuff that they've been handing you about how dangerous and terrible the world is, although you thought it was silly some of it sunk in and you believe some of it. I think you believe it with school. What do you think?

Patient: They never told me anything about it.

Therapist: No, but I think that the kind of tension and the scared feeling that you get when you're in school is very similar to what happens to your father when he's in restaurants and elevators. What do you think?

Patient: Maybe.

Therapist: Why do you think that I may be right? How might they be similar?

Patient: Because my father is afraid to go to a theater unless he sits in the back row.

Therapist: Hhmmm.

Patient: And I guess being afraid of, you know, going to a theater and all could be similar to me being afraid to go to school, but I don't know—

Therapist: Do you think that his fear of going into a theater is kind of silly?

Patient: Yes.

Therapist: What about your fear of going to school?

Patient: I guess it's silly, but I can't help it.

Therapist: I see. I know you can't help it just like he can't help it. But you know there's one thing that's important to remember here and that is that, as I see it, one of the reasons why you are so afraid of school is that this is part of what you've been told all these years about how dangerous various things are—you know, going out without sweaters and it's dangerous to cross the streets alone and you've been told by your father that elevators can be dangerous. Although he didn't say it, he was always afraid to go into closed places so you thought for a long time that there was something to be frightened about.

Patient: Yeah.

Therapist: So I think that you have been exposed to a lot of talk and action, talk and behavior that suggests that the world is a dangerous place. Hhmmm?

Patient: Uh huh.

Therapist: Do you think it's as dangerous as your parents see it?

Patient: No.

Therapist: Do you think that the school is as dangerous as you see it?

Patient: I don't know.

Therapist: Anything you want to say to me.

Patient: No.

Therapist: Hhmmm. Okay. Of all the things we've spoken about since your story, which do you think is the most important?
Patient: Since the story?
Therapist: Yes. Just now.
Patient: Not before? I guess about being afraid of things.
Therapist: What particular thing?
Patient: School.
Therapist: And what is the most important thing I said about that?
Patient: That it isn't as dangerous as I think I think.
Therapist: Hhmmm. What do you think about that?
Patient: I don't know.
Therapist: Do you think I'm right or not?
Patient: Uh huh. But I'm not really worried about the school being danger-ous, just nervous.
Therapist: Well, you're nervous. But what are you nervous about?
Patient: I don't know.
Therapist: Right. It's just like your father. Your father doesn't know what he's nervous about in theaters, does he?
Patient: I think he's afraid that if there's a fire or something and he won't be able to run out.
Therapist: What about elevators? Restaurants?
Patient: Oh, elevators. He's afraid that he's going to get stuck.
Therapist: But he knows that that's not likely.
Patient: Yeah.
Therapist: Okay.

In my story I reinforced the insights and therapeutic gains mani-fested in Bonnie's story. The parents admit that their fears are un-realistic, which makes it easier for the patient to accept their irra-tionality. I point out that there are some dangers in the world but not to the degree and severity her parents would have her believe. Also, she has the resources to protect herself and avoid some of these dan-gers: "They were pretty sensitive and when they would smell a hunter from a distance, before the hunter would even see them, they would get out of his way." In the ensuing discussion, I attempted to clarify on a conscious level Bonnie's awareness of her parents, dis-tortions.

The reader may wonder why, by the seventh month of treat-ment, I still hadn't gotten into the "deeper" psychodynamics with Bonnie—elements such as the unconscious anger she harbored toward her mother for the latter's rejection; her fear that such hostility would bring about her mother's death; and the determination to stay close to her to reassure herself that her mother was still alive. First, I must follow the patient's leads. Her stories, dreams, and conscious productions directed me to the material I have presented. A few attempts to "probe deeper" were met with significant resistance. Bonnie was not ready to deal with these issues, and it would have been anti-therapeutic to pursue them. Second, the conditioning elements were certainly contributing factors to her phobias and concentration on them was proving effective—there was no reason to spoil things. I could have woven these deeper problems into my stories, but to do so would have made them so remote from the issues in the patient's story that she could not have "grabbed" them. Lastly, as I have said, I do not belive that conscious understanding of one's psychodynamics is invariably necessary for clinical improvement.

Three days after the interchange just described, Bonnie related this story:

> Once upon a time there was this alligator family and they lived in the middle of the jungle and all the other animals, like the monkey and the parrots and all, were afraid of them because they thought that alligators were mean and that he was going to bite them.
>
> *Therapist*: The alligator family went into the middle of the jungle and all the other animals were afraid?
>
> *Patient*: Yes, because he was mean.
>
> *Therapist*: The animals were afraid of the alligator family?
>
> *Patient*: Yes. So the alligator family didn't have anybody who liked them. So they were very lonesome. Then one little monkey was walking along in the woods and he saw the little alligator. They started playing. They were about three or four or five years old. Then the mother was looking for her monkey and she saw him playing with that little alligator. So she grabbed him quickly and made him come and she thought that the alligators were going to hurt him. So then the little alligator said, "Why are you taking the monkey away?" She said, "Because you're going to eat him." He said, "No, I'm not." She said, "Yes, you are. All alligators eat other animals." He said, "No, they don't." Then the mother alligator came out, and she said, "Hello." They started to talk, I guess, and the monkey lady was still scared. But then after a while she wasn't scared anymore, and they were free and that's the end.
>
> *Therapist*: And after a while they weren't scared anymore. What's the moral of that story?
>
> *Patient*: If you think you're afraid of someone—if you don't know someone

you shouldn't say that they'll eat you or something because they might not. They might be friendly.

Therapist: Okay. Now let me ask you a question. What was it about the conversation between the mother monkey and the mother alligator that made the mother monkey less scared of the mother alligator?

Patient: Nothing. She just, while they were talking, the alligator didn't try to eat the monkey.

Therapist: She just saw that it didn't happen. Is that it?

Patient: Yeah.

Therapist: I see. So the mother monkey saw that it didn't happen. She had never had the guts to try before. Is that it? *(Bonnie nods affirmatively.)* Hhmmm. Okay. I want to ask you a question. Do you think this story has anything to do with your situation now?

Patient: No.

Therapist: Not at all? What about the fact that you are afraid of something, like going to school and that you're seeing that it isn't as scary as you thought that it might be?

Patient: I didn't think about that when I told this story.

Therapist: That's all right. Now that I've mentioned this to you, do you think there's something to what I am saying?

Patient: No.

Therapist: You don't think so. You don't think that there might be something similar between the mother monkey seeing that it's not so frightening to be with alligators and your—are you finding that things in school aren't as frightening as you thought that they might be?

Patient: No.

Therapist: You're not finding that out at all?

Patient: No.

Therapist: Okay. Well, thank you very much. Now it's time for me to tell my story.

The story is another attempt at fantasy desensitization—part of the working-through process. I believed Bonnie when she told me that she did not see any relationship between her story and the actual experiences of her life where she was far less phobic than she had been. A child's story will sometimes portray his or her life's situation with uncanny accuracy yet the child will have no conscious awareness of it. I did not, therefore, think that Bonnie here was "putting me on." But I did not believe her when she denied a lessening of her school fear. There was definite improvement (although she still had a way to go) and it was typical of her to exaggerate the horrors of school to discourage those who would urge her to go. One of her maneuvers was: "How can you be so cruel and force me to suffer such horrible tortures?" This is the story I told in response:

Once upon a time there was a family who lived in the woods and they were a monkey family. There was a mother monkey, a father monkey, and a little boy monkey. He was about five years old. Now this monkey mother and father were scared of a lot of things. For instance, the mother would say to the little monkey, "Now be very careful when you're outside. I don't want you climbing tall trees. If you climb tall trees, you'll fall off and you'll hurt yourself." Or she would say, "Now you don't walk on the coconut trees 'cause those coconuts will fall off and they'll hit you. Now don't you play with those rough kids that live over there down near the path because they're rough and they'll hurt you. I don't want you to get hurt. Now don't you stay out too late. You know, its dark and you'll get lost in the woods. Be careful." She was always telling this monkey how to watch out and be careful. She was always protecting him from all kinds of dangers that she saw in the forest.

Well, anyway, this monkey went out and he was playing with some of the kids. It got to be about five-thirty and he said, "I've got to run home." They said, "Why do you have to run home?" He said, "I have to get home before it gets dark." They said, "Why?" He said. "Well, I may get lost." They said, "How can you get lost? It's just a straight path from here to your house. It would be impossible to get lost." He said, "Well, isn't it dangerous at night in the jungle?" They said, "Ah, not particularly." Anyway, he began to talk to these other kids and he found out that many of the things that his mother was afraid of, they weren't. For instance, when he said, "Do you kids ever walk under coconut trees?" They said."Sure we walk under coconut trees." "Doesn't a coconut ever fall down on you?" he asked. They said, "Look that could happen once in a hundred years, that a coconut could fall down and hit you on the head while you are standing under the tree, but that doesn't mean that you should walk around constantly frightened that a coconut is going to fall on your head." He said, "Do you kids climb trees?" They said, "Of course. It's great fun." "But you might fall down and get hurt." "Yeah," they said, "once every few years somebody might slip and fall, but that's not a reason not to have all the fun of climbing trees." They scampered up the trees; they were jumping from tree to tree and swinging from the vines. That little monkey said, "Gee, I think I'm going to try that." He very carefully—he was kind of scared—he climbed up the side of the tree and he got onto a vine and he swung and wheee! Boy, did he have a good time swinging in the trees back and forth. He said, "Boy, what I've been missing all this time."

Well, he got home later on. It was after dark and his mother said, "Oh, I was so worried about you. Oh, my, I'm so glad to see my little baby boy. Come here. I want to kiss you." She hugged him and kissed him. She smothered his face and she kissed him and it got all wet. Ich! Anyway, she said, "Oh, my little baby boy. What happened to you? What were you doing out there?" "Oh," he said, "I was swinging on the trees." She said, "Swinging on the trees? Oh, my poor boy. Look at you. Look you have a little scratch on you arm." So he said, "Yeah, so what? So what? So I have a scratch on my arm. So what about that?" She said, "Oh, my little baby. Look at you. Your hair is all messed up. Oh! oh!"

Patient: (*Laughs appreciatively.*)

Therapist: What tree were you swinging from?" He said, "Oh, the big one down by the brook." "The big tree by the brook! Oh, my—how terrible." He said, "It's not so terrible, Ma. All the kids swing from that tree." She said, "I hope you didn't walk home under that row of—you know what kind of trees; I don't even want to say it."

Patient: Coconut trees.

Therapist: She said, "I hope you didn't walk under that row of coconut trees?" He said, "I did." "Let me look at your head. Maybe a coconut fell on your head." He laughed at his mother and said, "Look, Ma, there's no coconuts falling down. Once every hundred years maybe a coconut falls down while a kid is there, but that doesn't mean that there's any reason not to walk under coconut trees."

Well, when the father came home he was very upset too when he had heard about all the things that the boy had done. But the boy didn't listen to them anymore. He had learned his lesson from the other kids, and after that he was a much happier boy. Do you know what happened to his parents? What do you think happened to them?

Patient: I don't know.

Therapist: They got used to the idea and he used to then have a lot more fun. He would go out with the other kids. He would play with them. Sometimes they would be fighting—a little roughnecking once in a while. Sometimes he'd get scratched, but he had so much fun with them that he didn't mind doing that and he would swing through the trees. Sometimes they would even cut the coconuts down and they'd throw them at one another and they really had a wonderful time.

And you know what the lesson of that story is?

Patient: No.

Therapist: Try to figure it out.

Patient: That if your parents are really worried about you getting hurt you should ignore their crazy ideas.

Therapist: Yes, that the world has a few little dangerous things, but that doesn't mean you should deprive yourself of all the fun that you could have by doing all the things in the world. The world is less dangerous than many people think. The end.

      What do you think of that story?

Patient: I don't know.

Therapist: Do you have any thoughts about it?

Patient: No

Therapist: Did you like it?

Patient: Yes, very much.

Therapist: What was the part you liked the most?

Patient: When the monkeys were swinging through the trees.

Humor can be quite helpful in gaining the child's interest and thus increasing his receptivity to the therapist's story. Here, Bonnie was enraptured. She laughed heartily and clearly identified, in a deeply emotional way, with the monkey who dared defy his parents.

It was during this period of therapy that another issue arose that was crucial in Bonnie's treatment. I have already mentioned that her father was most interested in the occult and communication with the dead. Because he felt that discussing these matters would be anxiety-provoking to his daughter he never discussed them directly with her. However, his experiences in these areas were often a major topic of conversation. When Bonnie was present, her parents and their friends would speak about these subjects euphemistically. The whole area was shrouded in mystery to Bonnie, and even the most peripheral references to occult matters filled her with dread and would intensify a longstanding fearful preoccupation with ghosts.

Since I did not think that Bonnie herself was up to the task of convincing her father to discuss these matters with her, I decided that I would first meet with her father alone, in the hope that I could get him to initiate such a conversation. In our discussion he told me that his interest in communicating with the dead arose after his son from a former marriage had died of leukemia. He had visited a number of spiritualistic mediums with whom he had experiences that led him to believe that he was communicating with his dead son. He described a number of other experiences involving prediction of the future which confirmed his beliefs in these areas. I in no way felt that the father was psychotic and although I, myself, was incredulous about his experiences, I felt that they were attempts to maintain a relationship with a boy whose loss was probably the greatest trauma of his life. More than anything else, his belief in the occult was a manifestation of his love for his dead son.

I tried to explain to him that shrouding these matters in secrecy was contributing to Bonnie's anxieties and recommended that he discuss them openly with her. He flatly refused, claiming that they could only upset her more. I tried to explain to him that there was nothing intrinsically upsetting in his beliefs, and that if Bonnie were upset, it would only be because he believed that the revelations would be upsetting. None of his occult experiences had been anything but benevolent. He agreed that this was so and finally, with greatest hesitation and reluctance, agreed to discuss these matters with Bonnie, but in a family interview so I could be right there to "pick up the pieces." I agreed to this.

At the appointed time he asked to see me alone first, to be reassured that "I knew what I was doing." I told him that to the best of my knowledge this was a proper course and that even if I were mistaken, such revelations could not produce chronic psychiatric disorder; at worst only a little more acute anxiety. Bonnie and her mother were brought in and the father nervously told them the story of his interest in the occult, from the time of the death of his son (whom Bonnie did know about). On two occasions, he interrupted himself, turned to me and asked: "Are you sure you want me to go ahead Doctor? I think this is cruel." I urged him on. Bonnie was more anxious over her father's hesitation than about the actual material he revealed. By the end of the interview the father was surprised at Bonnie's calmness. I encouraged them all to continue the discussion at home and to answer as fully as possible any of Bonnie's questions.

During the next few weeks there was a further diminution in Bonnie's fears, and she was balking even less about going to school. In our sessions we spoke about the family interview with particular emphasis on these points: ignorance of a subject only increases one's anxiety over it and causes one to think that it is worse than it is; when one has the courage to face that which is anxiety provoking, it most often reduces one's fears; her father's interest in communicating with the dead arose from his desire to have some contact with the son he loved so much (just like he loves his daughter); and although she, herself, doesn't believe in such things, she can respect her father's belief.

About two weeks after the family meeting, at the beginning of her eighth month of treatment, Bonnie told this story:

> Once in this town there was this man and he lived in this house and everyone didn't like him because he'd never come out of the house and they'd think he was a witch or a monster or killed little kids or something. They made up all kinds of stories about him.
>
> So some kids one day said to some other kids that they didn't believe that he was really that mean. They, of course, thought that he was, but they were just trying to start an argument. So the other kid said, "Oh, yeah, well I heard from my grandmother that he ate his nephew or his dog or something." So then they really got mad and they began to figure out that nobody could be that bad. Then they kept trying to cause an argument like if he ate his nephew he'd be dead and all. So the little kid said, "I dare you to go and ring the doorbell on Halloween or something." So they got so mad at these other kids that they said, "All right if you really want it that way. Then we will."
>
> So him and his sister and his brother and his sister went to the house on Halloween. They rang the doorbell and they were all kind of scared and the other kids were waiting behind a tree. Then this little man opened the door or a lady or something and she said that she didn't have any candy to give them because nobody ever comes around. So they said, "Trick or treat," and they were all very scared and this person opened the door. She was very nice. She said she didn't have any candy because nobody ever came around her house, but she did give them money. She gave them about three dollars apiece and they found out that she was a really a nice lady. So then one of the kids asked her, "Why don't you ever come outside?" She said, "I come outside, but only in the backyard 'cause in the front yard it's too rocky for my feet. I'll fall 'cause I have weak ankles," or something like that. So they found out that she could only go in the backyard because there was nothing but grass there. It wasn't hard and she had a big flower garden.
>
> So she gave them a lot of money and the other kids because they thought she was so horrible didn't get half of the money. They got about two dollars all together, and they just got two dollars from her house. So the other kids who went there to see if she was nice or not found out to be the luckiest and the other kids weren't as lucky as the other kids. That's the end.

Therapist: What's the moral of that story?

Patient: That if someone tries to get into an argument with you and disagrees with you, you should put up a fight and try to prove that you're right and if you are you'll be a lot luckier; if you're not, well then it's not that bad, but if you are it's good.

Therapist: Any other morals to that story? That's one moral.

Patient: No

Therapist: See, the moral you gave pertains to the fact that the first group put up a fight against the second group to prove their point, but is there any moral about what their point was—about the old lady?

Patient: Oh, yes—that maybe if you don't just keep making up stories in your head that someone's bad. You should ask the person who you think is bad and if she does anything to you she'll probably get arrested anyway. So you shouldn't be that scared. The person probably could be nice to you if you go and ask her. She'll be your friend or something.

Therapist: I see. Now let me ask you this question. Why were they scared? Why did they think that there was some kind of a monster in that house or something like that? What gave them that idea?

Patient: 'Cause no one had ever seen her. They thought that she was just some lady who didn't want anyone to know that she was there.

Therapist: Why did they think that she was a monster? Because no one had ever seen her?

Patient: Well, they didn't think that she was really a monster, but they were kind of scared of her and I guess when people would ask other people what happened or why she never came out, the other people probably just made up stories about her.

Therapist: That she was a monster or what?

Patient: Oh, that she was mean to little kids or something.

Therapist: I see, just because they never saw her. I see. Okay.

Patient: That story I just made up. It kind of reminds me of "To Kill a Mockingbird."

Therapist: How so?

Patient: Have you ever read the book?

Therapist: Quite a long time ago. I don't remember much of it.

Patient: Well, there's this guy named Bradley. He lived in such an old house that they made up stories about him like he was chained to the bedpost and all. He came out and saved John's life.

Therapist: Hhmmm.

Patient: That's why it reminds me so much.

Therapist: I see. So what's the lessons to be learned about that?

Patient: I don't know. There could be a lot of different reasons why you shouldn't make up stories about people unless you really know them.

Therapist: Right. Right. Thank you very much. Now it's time for me to tell my story.

The story reiterates one of the important lessons Bonnie had learned during the previous two weeks: ignorance enhances anxiety. When you don't know something about a situation, you often think the worst. Her father's interest in the supernatural was secretively concealed and this, in itself, engendered in her the notion that "If it's too terrible to talk about, it must really be dreadful." In this story Bonnie describes the reputation for violence these recluses suffered because of their inaccessibility. Bonnie pushes through her fears, directly confronts the forbidden, and finds that the dangers existed in her own mind only. This is exactly what happened when she had the courage to discuss her father's involvement with the occult.

In response, I told this story:

Once upon a time a new family moved into a neighborhood and they moved next to this house. Now the parents of the child in the new family were kind of scared people. They were very suspicious of the world and they always thought the worst in every situation. They told their daughter on the very first day that they moved into town, "We don't want you visiting the next door neighbor's house." She said, "Why?" They said, "Just so. You'll never know what will happen. Who knows who the people might be and what kind of terrible things might happen to you. Stay away from them and you'll be safe." She said, "What's to be afraid of?" They said, "We don't know. Just play it safe. Don't go near there."

Well, this girl decided that she didn't know what her parents were talking about. She had seen a glimpse of the lady who lived in the house and she looked all right. So the next day when no one was around she went into the backyard of those people and it looked like a pretty nice backyard. She couldn't see anything wrong with it. Then she went out and she looked in the front yard. It looked all right. Then she went to the window and peeked in the window. She looked around and the people weren't home. She didn't see anything particularly unusual. Then suddenly behind her she heard a footstep. She turned around and it was the nice lady who owned the house. The lady said, "Hello. What are you doing here?" The little girl said, "I just moved into the neighborhood." So the lady said, "Well I'm very happy to have you here. Why didn't you come to the front door?" She said, "I don't know. My parents kind of told me that I should stay away and that there might be dangerous things here." She said, "I don't know whether it's dangerous, but the only criticism I have of you is that you didn't come up the front door. I don't particularly like people sneaking around my property, but outside of that I think if you come around here once in a while we'll be very happy to see you. Would you like to come in and have a cookie and some milk?"

So the little girl, having been told by her parents that things are dangerous and you should never trust people and things like that, was kind of scared at first, but she finally decided that her parents probably didn't know what they were talking about. So she went in and she had cookies and milk. This woman was a very good cook and she made very nice cookies. She had three of the most excellent and sweetest cookies you could imagine and then went home.

Her mother said, "Where were you this afternoon?" She said, "Promise you won't be angry at me?" Her mother said, "I don't know. Tell me where you were." She said, "I went to visit the people next door." Her mother said, "What? The people next door?" She said, "Yes." "Oh, you never listen to me. You're going to get into trouble." She said, "There's no trouble. They happen to be very fine people and I met the lady of the house and she gave me good cookies." "She gave you cookies. How were they?" She said, "They were fine. I liked them very much." Her mother said, "I hope you don't get sick." She said, "I'm not going to get sick. They were excellent cookies." Anyway, the next day the girl wasn't sick and then the mother and father began to realize that things weren't as bad over in that new house as they had thought and they even became friends with those people.

The lesson of my story is that many things that you think may be dangerous are not so, but the only way that you are going to find out is to look carefully and observe them and see what they are really like. Then you can decide whether or not they are dangerous. For example, this girl looked in the window to see what was really going on there, to see if there was anything dangerous. Most often things are not dangerous, but you think they might be dangerous if you do not know what's going on. However, knowing about a thing often makes you less scared. The end. Do you have any comments about this story?

Patient: No.

Therapist: Okay then. Very good.

My story merely reiterates the main themes presented in Bonnie's. The messages were important, reflected healthier thinking, and were, therefore, worthy of repetition.

Four days later, she told this story:

Once there was a frog and it was living in a little pond with just some other frogs. It was nice there and then all of a sudden, then one day snakes started coming in and lizards. They got the pond all dirty and messy and they'd fight.

So these frogs were unhappy and so they left that pond and they decided to go find another pond. So they walked around. So they looked and they came to a pond and there were a few snakes there. One of them said, "Gee, maybe this is a good pond." Then they saw a snake and they said, "Oh, I guess not." The snake said, "Why isn't this a good pond?" The frogs said, "Oh, because there's too many other snakes in it and lizards and all. We can't stay in a place like that." The snake said, "Why not?" They said, "We don't know. It just wouldn't work out. There's too many of you and there's just a few frogs. It just won't work out." The snake said to them that maybe if they lived there for a few days they might like it and decide that snakes and lizards aren't bad.

So they did and then all of a sudden the frogs started to like the snakes and lizards and all, and thought that this would be a fun place to live with all different kinds of animals. They did and they were happier than just being with just plain old frogs in one little pond.

Therapist: Hhmmm. And what's the lesson of that story?

Patient: That if you don't like other people and all, and you don't really know them, you should know them first and then see whether you like them

Therapist: In other words, know them first before deciding whether or not you like them.

Patient: Yeah.

Therapist: Very good. That was an excellent story. Now it's time for me to tell my story.

Slimy little animals, obnoxious creatures, and loathsome vermin most often symbolize unacceptable unconscious complexes. In this story, the frogs represent Bonnie and the snakes and lizards symbolize unconscious thoughts and feelings. Whereas she first fled from such complexes, her experiences in therapy have made her more comfortable with them, and the story dramatically reflects this. At a more superficial, but nonetheless meaningful, level the story reveals her increasing comfort with all the elements in her life that she once feared.

This is the story I told in response:

Once upon a time there were some frogs and they lived in a pond and then some snakes and lizards started moving into the pond. The older frogs kept telling the younger frogs that this place was becoming a terrible place to live in because of these snakes and lizards. They kept saying, "Snakes and lizards are no good. They are dangerous, terrible, and they bother people. They're really no good bums and everything else." So this kind of made these young frogs kind of scared of these snakes and lizards.

Then one day a wise old frog was passing by and he said "Why are you kids so frightened?" "Well," they said, "there are a lot of snakes and lizards moving around here." So the wise old frog said, "Well, what can they do to you?" They said, "We don't know. It's just that our parents tell us that these snakes and lizards are dangerous." He said, "Look, I'm a wise old frog and I've been living around here longer than your parents. I know the snakes and lizards quite well and there's really nothing to be afraid of with them. They're the usual things you find in any pond. I suggest you go out and play with them and you'll find that what I'm saying is true."

So, somewhat reluctantly and hesitatingly, the frogs decided to play with the snakes and lizards. To their surprise they found out that what the old wise frog had said was true—that these snakes and lizards were not such frightening things—and they became very good playmates and had a very good time.

Do you know what the lesson of that story is?

Patient: No.

Therapist: Try to figure it out.

Patient: That the animals weren't all that dangerous and mean and they shouldn't be that scared of them.

Therapist: Yes. And also not everything your parents may tell you about the dangers of an animal are necessarily true. Sometimes your parents say something about the dangers of certain animals that will not be true. The end.

Here, I reinforced Bonnie's message and added the element of her parent's contribution to her distortions.

Clinically, Bonnie was enjoying significant improvement. Following the family interview and during the ensuing discussions, there was a progessive diminution of her school-phobic symptoms. In addition, for the first time in years, Bonnie enjoyed a remission of her preoccupation with ghosts. She was now attending school every day and stayed throughout the day, with only occasional morning anxiety.

In the middle of her eighth month of treatment and one week after the sequence just presented, Bonnie told this story:

Once there was this kangaroo family and they lived in Australia and they had big places to run around and all. They had a lot of fun. One day the hunters came and they were going to take them back to this place in Florida called Jungleland. The kanagroos thought things like they were going to go to a zoo and be put in cages and have people stare at them and have no place to run around and just be in a little cage. But when they got there they found out that it was really like where they used to live—a big jungle and all—and they could run around and do everything they wanted. But there was one thing they didn't like. There were a lot of other animals in there and sometimes they wanted to stay in some special place and they found out that a giraffe was staying there or a lion, and they couldn't work anything out. They'd always fight.

So then one day the zookeeper said—well, not the zookeeper, but the man—said, "You animals are always fighting. You're always fighting about things. I don't know what you're fighting about, but you're always fighting. You should stop and I assure you you'll be a lot more happier in Jungleland." So the animals thought that he was a little crazy in telling them that they could get along with each other, but one lion said, "Maybe's he right. Maybe if we work out special places for us to stay, maybe we could be friends." So the giraffe said, "Well, I always liked the section by the tree." The kangaroos and all the other animals said, "Fine. That's all right." And the kangaroos said, "We always liked the section where it's very hot." And they said, "Fine, you can stay there." Then the lions said, "We like the section by the water." They said, "Fine. You can live there." They all had their own places to live and once in a while some other animal would go to the other animals to visit or spend the night or something. They all were friends after that. That's the end.

Therapist: And what's the lesson of that story?

Patient: That if you're always arguing with other people for what you want and all, you shouldn't just fight with them. You should work out—you should try to work out something that will make everybody happy.

Therapist: I see. Very good. Okay. Thank you very much. That was a very interesting story, unusual also. And now it's time for me to tell my story.

This is the kind of healthy story one sees in the pretermination phase of therapy. It is of interest that the antipathy among the animals does not have a fear element—it is one of anger over territorial conflict. The problem is solved in a civilized manner using discussion and compromise. I believe that in addition to earlier sources of hostility Bonnie now harbored anger toward her parents for their having inculcated in her so many anxiety-provoking notions. One could say that the story reflects repression of such anger—the animals separate to protect themselves from one another. However, even if this is so, there is no question also that it is handled in a most mature way: civilized discussion, compromise, and mutual coexistence. The zookeeper, of course, who mediates all this, symbolizes the therapist.

I told this story in response:

> Once upon a time there were some kangaroos who lived in Africa and they roamed the plains. I'm sorry, they lived in Australia and they roamed the plains and they really enjoyed themselves. There were lots of places to run around and they had lots of fun.
>
> One day they got some news that some hunters were around and that these hunters were rounding up some of the kangaroos to bring to Florida to a place called Jungleland. Well, some of the kangaroos when they heard this kind of made believe that it didn't happen. They didn't want to talk about it and they said, "Better not discuss it. Talking about it is just going to make it worse. So let's make believe it isn't happening." So they didn't discuss it and what do you think happened to them? How do you think they felt?
>
> *Patient:* I don't know.
>
> *Therapist:* Well, they got very scared because when they did think about it, not having any information at all, they just thought the worst. They thought there would be death and destruction. They thought terrible things would happen. They thought that they would be put in cages. They thought that they would be beaten mercilessly. They thought that they would be starved. They thought that they would really be treated terribly by the keepers. But since they didn't talk about it and since they didn't ask questions, they just thought the worst. That's often what happens when you don't talk about something that you're afraid of. You think that it's far worse than it usually is.
>
> But some others asked the hunters what it was really like in Jungleland, and they told them that it was a wide open place and that there are no cages and that the keepers there are especially trained to take care of animals, that there is an abundance of food, and that none of the animals are treated poorly. Any of the conflicts that the animals have are usually discussed openly and that they are settled by calm deliberation and conversation. Well, when they heard that, many of their fears were diminished significantly. Then when they actually went there —they were still frightened a little bit because it

was a new place and strange and everything. New places are always strange no matter how much information you have about them. They always produce a little bit of fear.

So they went to the new place and they found out it was just as described and that it wasn't frightening and they got used to it. Actually they were happier there than they were in their original place because it was so well taken care of.

Do you know what the lessons of that story are?

Patient: No.

Therapist: Try to figure them out. What are some of the lessons?

Patient: That you should ask to find out if you're going to like it or not.

Therapist: Because?

Patient: Because if you don't ask you just think worse things about what it will be like and you'll never know whether you'll be happy or unhappy.

Therapist: Right. When you don't know, you usually think things will be worse than they really will be. That's the first lesson. The second lesson is that another way to reduce fears is to actually have the experience and see that it's not as frightening as you thought it might be. And that's what happened to these kangaroos. The end.

Do you want to make any comments about that story or your story?

Patient: No.

Therapist: Okay. Do you want to listen to any of them?

Patient: All right if you want.

Therapist: Well, do you want to?

Patient: All right.

Therapist: Okay. Do you want to listen to both or yours or mine or what?

Patient: Mine.

Therapist: Do you want to listen to mine too?

Patient: Okay.

Sometimes, in the pretermination phase of treatment following a healthy story I will tell one which reiterates elements from previous stages of treatment because the patient's story does not lend itself to salutary modification. This is what I did here: I demonstrated again how knowledge and direct experience can be powerful weapons against anxiety, whereas denial and ignorance only enhance it. The kangaroos that chose not to discuss the impending move were filled with horrifying fears; those who gathered information remained calm, and when they saw that their new home was as it had been described by the hunters they were even more relaxed.

During the next week Bonnie was weaned from tranquilizers

and she still maintained her clinical improvement. Near the end of her eighth month of treatment, she told this story:

> Once there were these kids and they wanted to go to this movie. There were about six of them and they didn't have enough money. They only had enough for maybe one ticket. So they didn't think of what they could do, so they couldn't get past the door, where the man was, without a ticket. There was an exit that they could get in, but you could only get out from the inside. You couldn't get in from the outside. So they didn't know what to do. So they thought for a while and then one kid said, "Well, I'm going to get a ticket," 'cause he had enough money. Then the other kid who had enough money said, "I guess I'll get a ticket too, but if you go around to the exit I'll let you in." So they went around to the exit.
>
> *Therapist:* You mean the second kid went into the theater and opened up the exit door for the kids outside?
>
> *Patient:* Yeah. So they went into the exit.
>
> *Therapist:* You mean the two kids who had enough money?
>
> *Patient:* Yeah. They opened the door and all the kids came in. Then the man who worked in the theater saw them all coming in and went over and caught them. He said, "If you're going to do that you can't come in this movie theater for a whole week. Then after the week is up you can come in as long as you have money."
>
> So the kids couldn't go and see the movies for a week and they were very disappointed. They found out that they should have waited till they got money.
>
> *Therapist:* And the lesson of that story is?
>
> *Patient:* That if you want to go someplace, like to the movies, you shouldn't cheat about it. You should try to get money or earn it or something, but you shouldn't just cheat or go in without paying.
>
> *Therapist:* Okay. Thank you very much. Now it's time for me to tell my story.

Once again, the movie-television screen is utilized—the screen upon which the patient's unconscious is projected for therapeutic observation. The story reveals late treatment ambivalence about further confrontation with her unconsicous. The previous few weeks had been somewhat harrowing, what with all the talk about communication with the dead, ghosts, and extrasensory perception. Bonnie wants a rest, and so arranges to get suspended from the movie house for a one-week period. I did not believe that the illegal maneuvers in the story had anything to do with any psychopathic trends in Bonnie, but were rather convenient mechanisms for predictably getting banned from the movie house.

This is the story I responded with:

> Once upon a time there were six kids and they were talking and they said, "Gee, what are we gonna do? What are we gonna do today? We've got three days off from school, Friday, Saturday and Sunday." It was a holiday and they didn't know what to do. So someone said, "Hey, how about going to a movie?" Someone else said, "Yeah, what's playing?" Another kid said, "Oh, there's a very scary picture playing in the neighborhood." Another kid said, "Aw, that picture isn't so scary." Anyway they started to argue over whether the picture was scary or not, and most of them thought that it was scary and they said, "Oh, we'd never go to see that movie. It's pretty scary." Others said, "Oh, it isn't so scary." So they kept arguing over whether it was scary or not. Those who thought it wasn't scary said, "We're going to go this afternoon at two o'clock and all those who want to come can meet us at two o'clock in front of the movie house and we'll go in together."
>
> Well, see, there were six kids there. Two said it wasn't scary. There were two who said it was scary, and there were two who were in the middle. They *thought* that it wasn't scary but inside they *felt* that it was. In other words, there were two parts to them. Their conscious minds thought it wasn't scary, but their unconsious minds thought that it was scary. Do you follow that?

Patient: Yes.

Therapist: Now those two kids in the middle group whose conscious minds thought that it wasn't scary said, "Okay, we'll go with you. We'll join you at two o'clock." But their unconscious minds thought that it was scary. So they found that they weren't that interested in going to the movies, even though they thought they were. At first they couldn't find the money that they were supposed to have in order to go to the movies. Then they forgot the time and had to call up their friends and see what time it was. Then they realized that because of the fact that they forgot the time and because of the fact that they forgot their money that maybe they were a little more scared than they had thought. Do you understand that?

Patient: Yes.

Therapist: Well, anyway, they decided to try it anyway. They figured that it can't be that bad and they'd try it. So anyway the four kids finally convinced the other two who really said they were scared to try going into the movie anyway and seeing what it was like. They said, "You can go out if you want, if you're really scared."

> Well, all six of them went in and, of course, some of them were a little scared at times, but all of them stayed and saw the whole movie

and they realized that there was far less to be scared about than they had thought. The two who weren't scared at first said to the others, "See, it wasn't as scary as you thought." The two who were very scared said. "Yes, you're right. It isn't as scary as we had thought." The two who were in the middle, who thought that they weren't scared, but really were, said, "I guess we were a little scared, but we're glad we went anyway because we found out that it wasn't so scary."

Do you know what the lesson of that story is?

Patient: No.

Therapist: Try to figure it out.

Patient: That things aren't as scary as you think?

Therapist: Yes. Things may not be as scary as you think initially and if you try it out, you often will find out that things aren't as scary as you thought in the beginning. The end.

In this story I provided Bonnie with a few lessons in elementary psychology while trying to assuage her fears of gaining further insight into her problems.

Clinically, the patient continued to do well. During her ninth month of treatment, Bonnie told a story about a fairy who wins wings for not having a bad word to say about anyone. Although that story certainly pertained to the unconscious anger she felt toward her parents, there had been such significant improvement in all areas of functioning (including definite, but less dramatic, improvement in expressing hostility) that I did not consider much more work with her to be warranted.

This story was told one week prior to the date of discontinuation of treatment.

Once there was this dragon a long time ago and all the other dragons had wings and they could fly around, but this one was a little baby. He was about two or three years old and he didn't have his wings all grown yet, but he still wanted to fly. All of his other friends tried with their little wings and some of them did get off the ground; but he wanted to fly but he was afraid to get off the ground. So his parents also told him, "If you fly you'll get caught up in a tree or you'll fall and break your neck." Well, he really wanted to fly because he saw by his other friends how much fun it was, but he was still scared and very nervous about it. He thought it looked like fun, but he wasn't sure because he thought he might hurt himself.

So then his grandfather came over one day and he said to him, "I'll teach you how to fly if you want. You're old enough." The dragon said, "Well, I don't know. It's kind of dangerous. I better wait until I'm older." "Nonsense," said his grandfather. "All of your other cousins fly. Some of them even go up as high as clouds." So he thought, "Boy, going up as high as clouds. That's fun." "Well," he said, "my parents won't let me." His grandfather said, "Why don't you ask them?"

So they went to his parents and his grandfather said, "Why don't you let me teach him how to fly?" The parents said, "Teach him how to fly, are you kidding, at his age? He'll crash; he'll hurt himself; he'll break his neck; he'll never be able to get down; he'll get caught in a tree." They named a whole lot of terrible things. This made the little dragon even more frightened.

One time in the middle of the night the grandfather was staying for a month because his cave was being built over. So he woke up the little dragon and said: "Your parents are asleep. I'll teach you how to fly." He said, "Oh, no. I'll crash." So the grandfather took the little dragon and put him on his back. Then the grandfather ran out before he had time to get off and started flying. Up in the air went the grandfather with his little grandson on his back. Then the grandfather tilted a little so that the little dragon could fall off and the little dragon was flapping his wings very hard and slowly coming to the ground. Then as he almost reached the ground he started to flap a lot harder. Even if he touched the ground he couldn't have hurt himself because he was flapping so hard that he came down softly; but he flapped so hard that finally he got up in the air. He went up and up and he never wanted to come down. He flew around and he got up high and he played and his grandfather went up in the air. They had flying races and he never had any more fun in his life.

So then he showed his parents the next morning. He said, "Mommy, Daddy, I know how to fly." They were so scared and they got furious at the grandfather and they said, "What are you trying to do—kill our little boy?" and things like that. So when the little boy got up in the air he flew and he flew and he flew and they decided that maybe it wasn't as dangerous as they thought and that maybe they should let him fly. He's old enough and it's not really dangerous. That's the end.

The moral of that story is: You shouldn't be afraid of things like that and you should try them once and then if you find that they are dangerous then not try them again. You should always try. Usually things aren't as dangerous as people say they are or believe they are.

Therapist: Do you think there's any relationship between that story and anything that has happened to you?

Patient: Well, my parents were afraid of some things with me.

Therapist: What were they afraid of?

Patient: Oh, for me to swim in the deep end of our swimming pool; for me to cross the street or ride my bicycle off the circle. I couldn't do that for a long time.

Therapist: What else?

Patient: A lot of things. They were just afraid for me to do things.

Therapist: And now?

Patient: Well, some things they are not so afraid of me doing anymore, but they still are overprotective.

Therapist: When you were telling this story were you aware that the little dragon in the story was similar to you?

Patient: Well, I didn't think about it until later.

Therapist: You mean until after the story was over?

Patient: Oh, around the middle of the story.

Therapist: Then you realized it was like you?

Patient: Yeah, that his parents were afraid for him to do certain things that were just a tiny bit dangerous.

Therapist: So what's the main things that helped this dragon stop being afraid?

Patient: When he tried it.

Therapist: He tried it, uh huh. And what was the other thing—anything else that helped him not to be afraid?

Patient: Well, his grandfather took him out and showed it to him.

Therapist: I would say another thing was that he began to realize that the things his parents thought were not true.

Patient: Yes.

Therapist: That's very important that he began to realize that what his parents thought were frightening things were not frightening things for him. Hhmmm?

Patient: Yes.

Therapist: I see. Okay. Well, that was an excellent story. Do you think there's any story that I can make up that could improve upon yours?

Patient: Maybe that his grandfather didn't show him. He showed himself.

Therapist: It's going to be hard to improve upon that story, isn't it? That he did it on his own; that's a good idea. I would say that my story would say that gradually as he got older—let's say that we don't have his grandfather in the story—he realized that the things his mother and father were saying were not so because he saw that other mothers and fathers were saying different things and his friends were doing these things and they were not in any kind of trouble so he tried it himself even though it was scary at first.

So what do you think about your troubles about being afraid to do things? Do you still think you have that trouble or not?

Patient: I'm not—no—not particularly.

Therapist: I don't think so either. Tell me, if you weren't moving to Col-

orado, in a couple of months, do you think you would be able to stop
seeing me?

Patient: I suppose so.

Therapist: Yes, that's what I think. What about next week? Do you think
you should come next week?

Patient: It doesn't matter to me.

Therapist: Do you want to come just for old times' sake—since it's your last
week?

Patient: Okay.

Therapist: Okay. Very good.

As Bonnie tells us herself, during the first part of her narrative
she was not consciously aware that the story pertained to her. That
she did relate it to herself in the latter part does not, in my opinion,
lessen the story's validity. This was not the kind of child who "buttered me up."

The patient herself provided a suggested improvement, obviat-
ing the need for me to tell a story. Discussion of the plot of a story
incorporating her refinement was sufficient.

During the same session, Bonnie related a dream from the previous night:

> I was with this skin diver. There was a lady and a man with us too. We
> were standing on a dock, ready to dive. I was scared at first; but we
> dived off into the bay. It was at night. We swam across the water to
> another dock. We got up on the other dock. There was a houseboat
> there and we had dinner in it. I wasn't scared anymore.

Bonnie had had some experience with me in dream analysis
and thought that the two adults represented her parents and the skin
diver, the therapist. She surmised that the diving into the water
stood for her treatment, where she and her parents had learned to do
many things which they had previously found anxiety provoking.
Swimming across the bay symbolized the successful completion of
the therapeutic course. Enjoying a good meal represented her new
freedom to enjoy the pleasures of the world.

The dream and story each supported my clinical decision that
Bonnie was ready to leave. Bonnie's termination story was told at
her next-to-last session. During nine months of treatment, Bonnie
had sixty-two sessions. Her story about the grandfather who helped
the little dragon learn how to fly in spite of the protests of her parents
epitomized her treatment. Her termination dream about the skin
diver, who led Bonnie and her parents through the "scary" waters to

safety on the other side of the bay, confirmed my clinical decision to terminate treatment.

The reader may wonder why this girl improved without working through the basic anger toward her mother which is often central in the separation anxiety disorder. I believe that Bonnie, like many other children with this problem, feared separation from her mother because she needed to be reassured that her unconscious death wishes toward her mother would not be realized. The anger, in part, relates to deprivation fears and this was certainly the situation with Bonnie as she revealed in her first story about the abandoned kitten. Also, as is so often the case in the families of children with school phobia, the parents have phobias as well, and these contribute to the formation of the symptom. In Bonnie's family this element was of paramount importance. Other factors as well are often operative and each child must be evaluated separately to determine which ones contribute to his or her fear of school.

The stories that the child tells in the storytelling game are a valuable source of information in determining the psychodynamics of any particular child's phobia. They provide the therapist with the leads to follow in the therapeutic work. Those who criticize *The Mutual Storytelling Technique* as being too manipulative and coercive should appreciate that it is not done haphazardly and casually. The child's lead is followed. If, like all other forms of psychotherapy, *The Mutual Storytelling Technique* is "brainwashing," at least the patient gives the therapist clues as to what part of his brain to wash and when. Bonnie's stories and other productions led me to an approach which emphasized desensitization and correction of the phobia-engendering notions that had been inculcated by her parents and grandmother. Improvement in these areas seemed to be enough at that time. There is no point continuing treatment of a child who is relatively asymptomatic because the therapist sees evidence of further difficulties in the patient's fantasies, dreams, and stories.

With Bonnie there was some additional improvement of the basic deprivational problem as well. Bonnie did become more assertive in getting her parents to spend more time with her. She learned that the expression of her resentment in this area was not only effective in getting her more time with them, but she also learned that they did not respond punitively to her protestations. She had living experiences that angry thoughts were acceptable and did not harm anyone. These factors also, I believe, contributed to the resolution of her separation anxiety disorder.

7

Termination

GENERAL COMMENTS ABOUT TERMINATION

For many years I have been dissatisfied with the concept of termination as it is viewed by most psychoanalysts. The criteria for making the decision as to whether or not a patient should leave treatment are usually based on two considerations: 1) the degree of alleviation of symptoms and 2) the degree to which projective material (dreams, projective tests, play fantasies) reveal freedom from psychopathology. Psychoanalysts, especially, are often less concerned with improvements in area one than they are in area two. When there is symptomatic improvement and the second category reveals pathological processes, a patient may be encouraged to remain in treatment in order to be sure that the problem has been completely "worked through." In adult analysis, especially, one looks for a "termination dream"—a dream that suggests strongly that the problems have not only been worked through, but that the patient is ready to leave treatment.

I believe that the primary criteria for deciding whether or not therapy should terminate should be the patient's symptoms. Information obtained from area two sources may be highly revealing with regard to underlying psychodynamics but, I believe, it is often of little value in revealing whether or not a symptom is indeed present. If a symptom is present then one points to the psychodynamics for the explanation. In such cases things seem to fit together. However, we all have psychodynamics and all psychodynamics reveal a certain degree of inappropriate and maladaptive ways of dealing with life situations. When there are no particular symptoms, what does one do with the psychodynamics? I believe that many psychoanalysts do not fully appreciate the implication of what I have just said. What ultimately happens, I believe, is that the patient provides (often unconsciously) that projective material that will justify to both the analyst and the patient that termination is indeed appropriate. It is at that point that the patient had better "get out quickly" before new dreams appear that will inevitably reveal psychopathological processes. It is at that point that the analyst had better write his or her article if it is to demonstrate a "complete" analysis.

The whole concept of termination is, I believe, artificial. Life is filled with problems and there will always be new difficulties arising in anyone's life. The vast majority of projections include resolutions that could be considered inappropriate, maladaptive, or pathological. It is only in extreme cases that we can say with certainty that a particular dream is pathological. It is very difficult to differentiate the dreams of psychotics from the dreams of neurotics and the dreams of the so-called "normal" people. Accordingly, the use of projective material for determining when therapy should end is artificial and, I believe, could result in people being retained in treatment unnecessarily. I believe the best position for the therapist to take is one that is similar to that of the general medical practitioner. The patient comes when there is difficulty and continues treatment until the difficulties are alleviated to a significant degree. At that point the physician tells the patient not to hesitate to return if there is any further trouble either with that particular difficulty or with others. In such cases the patient does not feel humiliated or embarrassed when there is a continuation of the problem or when new problems arise. People who have had their analyses "terminated" are less likely to return with such a degree of comfort. In addition, the analyst him- or herself may be similarly reluctant to reinstitute treatment because it suggests that the previous analysis was somehow deficient.

Psychotherapy (of which psychoanalysis is one type) is a life experience that hopefully enriches and expands one's horizons. It is one of many life experiences that can provide such growth and these can punctuate our lives. When someone asks me when the therapy of most of my patients terminate with certainty, I usually say: "When one of us dies." But even then the therapy may not truly be terminated. If it turns out that I am the one to die first (and this is more likely because I am older than most of my patients), the treatment may still continue in that the patient may from time to time think about what went on in the therapy and find useful the things that have been said. So the true answer to that question is: "After both of us have died one can say that the therapy will have truly been terminated."

TERMINATION IN THE SEPARATION ANXIETY DISORDER

Because the separation anxiety disorder is so often a discrete symptom, it is often easier to determine when therapy should be terminated than in the treatment of other psychogenic disturbances. In short, I believe that treatment should be terminated when the child is going to school with the same degree of comfort as other children his or her age. However, one must also assess the situation with regard to the presence of other symptoms—especially in the area of dependency on an overprotective mother and the associated symptoms discussed in Chapter One. If the therapist has been successful in reducing to a significant degree the mother's overprotectiveness and, in addition, if the child exhibits only those dependencies that are age appropriate, then one can say that this problem no longer requires treatment. In addition, if there are no other symptomatic manifestations of any significance, then there are no longer any target symptoms. Such a child, like all other human beings on earth, is still likely to have fantasies that may reveal pathological processes. In fact, some of the fantasies might even reveal residual dependencies. This should not be surprising in that the pattern has been a deep-seated one. It has been the child's *modus vivendi* from the beginning of life, and it is not likely that other modes of adaptation are going to quickly fill the psychic life. And even when such other modes do appear, some of them are likely to be pathological as well. Our fantasies provide us with magic solutions. They gratify that which might not possibly be realized in reality. They provide compensations for life's deprivations. They provide denial, reaction formation, displacement, and a wide variety of other defense mechanisms. In short, most of the children who leave treatment with me have residual fantasies that might be viewed as pathological. Termination of my patients occurs when there is significant symptomatic alleviation over a reasonable period of time.

Clinical Example -- Pam

Pam's treatment demonstrates a number of the aforementioned principles. She first came into treatment at the age of 7, when she was in the first grade, with classical school-phobic symptoms. She was an only child and was overindulged and pampered by her parents, her maternal grandparents, and her maternal great grandmother—all of whom lived close to her home. There were no siblings, cousins, and other "rivals" in her area for the affection of all these individuals. She was generally looked upon as "the apple of everyone's eye." Furthermore, the family hesitated to place pressures on Pam in any area in which she showed resistance. For example, they had not sent her to day camp because she expressed hesitation over the prospect of going and they believed that it would be detrimental to her to pressure her into attending. She tended to view any restriction or reprimand as "yelling" and so the parents tried to avoid any criticism. In her whole life, her parents had never separated from her for a single day. Furthermore, they had discouraged her from sleeping over at other children's homes or going off with relatives and friends on such events as overnight camping trips.

Her original course of treatment lasted a little more than three months. In this case the parents did respond to counseling, and their needs to overprotect were not that deep seated that I had significant difficulty altering their child-rearing patterns. Pam too was receptive to therapy, and although there were hard times and much anger exhibited toward me for my recommendations, she basically was involved and receptive.

Two years later, at the beginning of the school year, Pam returned with an exacerbation of the original symptoms. This was in association with her getting a new teacher who had generally been considered to be strict and demanding. Pam had requested that her mother ask the principal to change her to another classroom, and

I discouraged such transfer. After three to four weeks of treatment Pam was once again comfortable in the new classroom. During the next six weeks she was basically asymptomatic. In accordance with my policy regarding termination, I suggested we consider discontinuing treatment. In the session that was scheduled to be her last, I asked her to draw a picture and then tell me a story. She drew a picture which contained two homes, a mother, and a girl named Joan. This is the story she told.

> This is a picture of a mother and a daughter. They're looking to buy a new house. They lived in this pink house over here. And they were thinking about buying this black and brown house over here. As they were going to the new house it started to rain and thunder. The girl thought the black and brown house was haunted. And she told her mother that she wasn't going to go in there. The mother said, "Go in there and I'll be right in." The girl went in first and said to her mother that she found ghosts in there and witches. So she ran out.
>
> So then they went home and the mother said, "We're going home." So then they got home and the mother said, "We're not going to buy a new house because everyone I try to pick out is not suitable." So they didn't get a new house.
>
> So three weeks later the girl told her mother that the house wasn't haunted. She said it was haunted because she didn't want to leave her old house. So they stayed in the old house.
>
> And the lesson of that story is: Don't play tricks on your parents.

I considered the story to be a reflection of residual fears of separation. Like most children with separation anxiety disorder, Pam feared new situations. And, like most children with separation anxiety disorder, they are not above fabricating in the service of avoiding such anxieties. Although the moral warns that one should not "play tricks" on (lie to) one's parents, this caveat does not obviate the basic message of the story. It is a typical bit of reaction formation that one commonly sees in the morals of many children's stories. In response, in the pattern of *The Mutual Storytelling Technique,* I told this story.

> Once upon a time a girl and her mother went looking for a new house. The family was growing and they needed a bigger house. Well, they came to this black and brown house which was really beautiful. The mother liked it very much. But the girl was scared to move from her

old house. It was familiar and she knew everything in the old house. The new house felt strange to her. She got scared about the idea of moving and really didn't want to move. So she went into the house first and then came running out and told her mother that the house was haunted and there were ghosts in there. Her mother said, "That's a lot of nonsense. There's no such thing as a haunted house. There's no such thing as ghosts. There's absolutely nothing to be afraid of about this house."

And so the mother then went into the house, but the girl was still scared to go in and she stayed outside. A few minutes later the mother came out and said that there was absolutely nothing to be afraid of about that house and she insisted that the girl go in. So the girl was scared at first and she went in with her mother. After a while she got less and less scared. Then she realized that her mother was right, that there was nothing to be scared about. The more she got to know about the house, the less scared she was.

Then they went home and made plans to move. Because the girl was still somewhat scared, they used to go visit the house every few days. Each time she visited she got less and less scared. The more she learned about the house, the more familiar it became, the less scared she was. Finally, when the day came to move, she wasn't even scared at all. Then she was embarrassed and even ashamed that she had told her mother that big lie about the ghosts and the haunted house.

And the lesson of my story is: If you're afraid of something at first, you'll be less scared the more information you have about the thing. Also, the more times you do a new thing, the less scared you'll be about it.

My responding story is typical of the kind that I tell children with separation anxiety disorder. It encourages desensitization and the acquisition of knowledge. Although the patient's story reflected residual separation anxieties, I did not consider it warranted to change my original recommendation that treatment be discontinued.

The patient was then given a second piece of paper and asked to draw another picture to which I requested a self-created story. This time she drew a picture of a house, four children, a tree, and a sun. This is the story she told.

One day the older brother, who was 12, decided to have a clubhouse. The younger brother felt bad because everybody else got more attention. So he climbed the tree into the clubhouse to get more attention up there. But he didn't get too much attention. Then he fell and hurt his arm. Then everybody gave him attention because of his broken arm. He was sick in bed and that gave him even more attention.

Then they bought him a bird. He went down to the kitchen to eat breakfast and he let the dog out and the dog let the bird out of the cage. He stopped eating and ran outside and got the bird. The mother and father then said, "I want some explaining."

So he said that "You love all the brothers and sisters more than me and I want more attention." The mother and father hugged him and tried to give him more attention. But they also punished him because he hurt his arm to get attention and let out the bird to get attention. So they didn't let him play. He had to stay in the house for a whole week because of what he did. The end.

The story reflects the patient's desire to utilize inappropriate ways of getting extra attention from her parents. Although, as mentioned, she had no siblings, the story does reflect rivalry with anyone else to whom the parents might give attention. The utilization of the broken arm to gain parental attention is reminiscent of the patient's utilization of somatic symptoms each morning. They not only served the purpose of her avoiding school, but gained parental attention as well. The patient appreciates somewhat the pathological adaptation revealed here in that the parents punish her for her inappropriate attention-getting maneuvers. With this understanding of Pam's story, I told this story.

Once upon a time there was a boy. He thought that his parents were not giving him as much attention as his brothers and sisters. Actually, they were. Actually, they loved all the brothers and sisters the same. But this boy thought the parents loved the others much more than they loved him.

So he began thinking of different ways of getting more attention. His older brother had built a tree house, and he thought that it would be a good idea to go up there and then fall out. He thought that if he then hurt his arm he would get a lot of attention. A kid in his class had broken his arm, and everybody had written their names on his cast. The thought of his lying in bed and everybody showing him sympathy really made him feel good. So he went up to the tree house and was ready to jump out when his older brother, a teen-ager, saw what he was doing. His brother quickly got up there and stopped him. His brother said, "What the hell are you doing? Are you trying to jump out of this tree house, or something?"

The boy then began to cry. He was ashamed of what he was trying to do, but had to admit to his brother that he was. He told his brother that he thought that he wasn't getting enough attention.

The brother then said, "Our parents love you as much as they love all the other kids. However, you're kind of quiet and don't do as many things as other people. You would get more attention if you hurt yourself by jumping out of this tree house. But you would pay a heavy price for that attention. You might break an arm or a leg and might even have to go to the hospital. In fact, you might even have gotten killed. I think you'd better think of other ways to get attention, ways that aren't going to hurt you, but ways that are going to make you a better person."

So the younger brother thought and asked if he could help the older brother build a new part on to the tree house. The older brother thought that would be a great idea. So the two of them then worked together for a long time and they really improved the tree house. Then everybody admired the younger brother, as well as the older brother. Actually, the younger brother did a lot of important work and many people found it hard to believe that he could have done such a good job on his own. Then he really felt good about the attention he got and didn't have to hurt himself in order to get it.

The message of my story is clear. I suggest healthy and appropriate attention-getting maneuvers rather than pathological ones. As is typical of my stories, I not only point out the drawbacks of the pathological adaptation, but introduce healthier alternatives that provide salutary gratifications in their own right. As mentioned, it is an old principle of treatment that you cannot take something away from someone without providing something attractive in return. Otherwise, the efforts are likely to prove futile.

Then the patient told me about a dream that she had had the previous night: "I took my bike into school and into the classroom. And my teacher said, 'Bring your bike home and then come back to school. You can't keep your bicycle in the classroom.' My teacher said it was okay to go home. So I went home. Then I woke up." I considered the dream to reflect residual separation anxieties. The bike serves, in part, as a transitional object. However, on the positive side, it is also a vehicle that enables her to leave her home and therefore has this positive implication as well. The inappropriateness of the bicycle in the classroom provides the teacher with a justification for sending the child home. Accordingly, the patient can say it is not she who wishes to leave the school, but she is merely following the teacher's instructions. The dream ends with her being at home, thereby satisfying her desire to avoid the school situation.

I am sure that some readers believe that the presentation of these three themes in the final session suggests strongly that therapy should not have been discontinued at that point. I am in disagreement. As mentioned, the patient had been symptom free for six weeks. She was functioning well in all areas and did not exhibit any clinical manifestations of separation anxiety. I believe the projective material presented in the final session reflected residual working through that did not *require* significant participation on my part. I am not saying that further sessions might not have been useful. I am not saying that I could not have continued to provide some useful messages of the kind provided in this final session. We all exhibit pathological manifestations from time to time and can all profit from advice and recommendations from those more knowledgeable than ourselves in a particular area. What I am saying is that after basic principles have been laid down and after there has been clinical improvement for a reasonable period of time (and I believe that six weeks was reasonable in this child's case) that one need not continue regular sessions. Without symptoms there is less motivation on both the parents' and the child's part to continue. And this can result in everyone's "souring" on therapy and make it less likely that the child will return in the future if it proves necessary. Once the principles have been introduced and once the child is showing definite evidence for their utilization—especially if there are no symptoms— then there is less need for a therapist. The changes in the underlying psychic structure are, I believe, last to take place. And these changes can take months and even years to be realized fully, and do not necessarily require the assistance of a therapist.

The session ended with my advising the mother and child that they should not hesitate to come back to me should there prove to be further difficulties. At the time of this writing, three years later, there have been no further problems.

References

Coolidge, J. C., Tessman, E., Waldfogel, S., and Miller, M. L. (1962), Patterns of aggression in school phobia. In: *The Psychoanalytic Study of the Child,* Vol. XVII, pp. 319–333. New York: International Universities Press.

Conn, J. H. (1939), The child reveals himself through play. *Mental Hygiene,* 23(1):1–21.

—— (1941a), The timid, dependent child. *Journal of Pediatrics,* 19(1):1–2.

—— (1941b), The treatment of fearful children. *American Journal of Orthopsychiatry,* 11(4):744–751.

—— (1948), The play-interview as an investigative and therapeutic procedure. *The Nervous Child,* 7(3):257–286.

—— (1954), Play interview therapy of castration fears. *American Journal of Orthopsychiatry,* 25(4):747–754.

Diagnostic and Statistical Manual of Mental Disorders (DSM-III) (1980). Washington, D.C.: American Psychiatric Association.

Eisenberg, L. (1958), School phobia: A study of communication and anxiety. *American Journal of Psychiatry,* 114:712–718.

Gardner, R. A. (1968), The Mutual Storytelling Technique—Use in alleviating childhood oedipal problems. *Contemporary Psychoanalysis,* 4: 161–177.

—— (1969), Mutual storytelling as a technique in child psychotherapy and psychoanalysis. In: *Science and Psychoanalysis*, ed. J. Maserman, Vol. XIV, pp. 123–135. New York: Grune and Stratton.

—— (1970a), Die Technik des wechselseitigen Geschichtenerzählens bei der Behandlung eines Kindes mit psychogenem Husten. In: *Fortschritte der Weiterentwicklung der Psychoanalyse*, ed. C. J. Hogrefe, Vol. 4, pp. 159–173. Göttingen: Verlag fur Psychologie.

—— (1970b), The Mutual Storytelling Technique: Use in the treatment of a child with post-traumatic neurosis. *American Journal of Psychotherapy*, 24:419–439.

—— (1970c), *The Boys and Girls Book About Divorce*. New York: Jason Aronson.

—— (1971a), Mutual storytelling: a technique in child psychotherapy. *Acta Paedopsychiatrica*, 38(9):253–262.

—— (1971b), *Therapeutic Communication with Children: The Mutual Storytelling Technique*. New York: Jason Aronson.

—— (1971c), *The Boys and Girls Book About Divorce*, Paperback edition. New York: Bantam Books.

—— (1972a), "Once upon a time there was a doorknob and everybody used to make him all dirty with their fingerprints. . . ." *Psychology Today*, 5(10):67–92.

—— (1972b), The Mutual Storytelling Technique in the treatment of anger inhibition problems. *International Journal of Child Psychotherapy*, 1(1):34–64.

—— (1972c), Little Hans—the most famous boy in the child psychotherapy literature. *International Journal of Child Psychotherapy*, 1(2): 24–50.

—— (1973a), *The Mutual Storytelling Technique* (12 one-hour audio cassette tapes). Cresskill, New Jersey: Creative Therapeutics.

—— (1973b), *The Talking, Feeling, and Doing Game*. Cresskill, New Jersey: Creative Therapeutics.

—— (1973c), *Understanding Children—A Parents Guide to Child Rearing*. Cresskill, New Jersey: Creative Therapeutics.

—— (1974a), La technique de la narration mutuelle d'historettes. *Médecine et Hygiène* (Geneva), 32:1180–1181.

—— (1974b), Dramatized storytelling in child psychotherapy. *Acta Paedopsychiatrica*, 41(3):110–116.

—— (1974c), The Mutual Storytelling Technique in the treatment of psychogenic problems secondary to minimal brain dysfunction. *Journal of Learning Disabilities*, 7:135–143.

—— (1974d), Psychotherapy of minimal brain dysfunction. In: *Current Psychiatric Therapies*, ed. J. Masserman, Vol. XIV, pp. 15–21. New York: Grune and Stratton.

—— (1975a), *Psychotherapeutic Approaches to the Resistant Child*. New York: Jason Aronson.

—— (1975b), *Psychotherapeutic Approaches to the Resistant Child* (2 one-hour audio cassette tapes). Cresskill, New Jersey: Creative Therapeutics.

—— (1975c), Techniques for involving the child with MBD in meaningful psychotherapy. *Journal of Learning Disabilities,* 8(5):16–26.

—— (1975d), Psychotherapy in minimal brain dysfunction. In: *Current Psychiatric Therapies,* ed. J. Masserman, Vol. XV, pp. 25–38. New York: Grune and Stratton.

—— (1976), *Psychotherapy with Children of Divorce*. New York: Jason Aronson.

—— (1979a), Helping children cooperate in therapy. In: *Basic Handbook of Child Psychiatry,* ed. J. Noshpitz, Vol. III, pp. 414–433. New York: Basic Books.

—— (1979b), Psychogenic difficulties secondary to MBD. In: *Basic Handbook of Child Psychiatry,* ed. J. Noshpitz, Vol. III, pp. 614–628. New York: Basic Books.

—— (1980), The Mutual Storytelling Technique. In: *The Psychotherapy Handbook,* ed. R. Herink, pp. 408–411. New York: New American Library.

—— (1981), The Mutual Storytelling Technique and dramatization of the therapeutic communication. In: *Drama in Therapy,* ed. G. Schattner and R. Courtney, pp. 211–235. New York: Drama Book Specialists.

—— (1983a), Treating oedipal problems with The Mutual Storytelling Technique. In: *Handbook of Play Therapy,* ed. E. E. Schaefer and K. J. O'Connor, pp. 355–368. New York: John Wiley & Sons.

—— (1983b), The Talking, Feeling, and Doing Game. In: *Handbook of Play Therapy,* ed. C.E. Schaefer and K.J. O'Connor, pp. 259–273. New York: John Wiley & Sons.

Gittelman-Klein, R. and Klein, D. F. (1973), School phobia: Diagnostic considerations in the light of imipramine effects. *Journal of Nervous and Mental Diseases,* 156(3):199–215.

Gittelman-Klein, R. (1975), Pharmacotherapy and management of pathological separation anxiety. *International Journal of Mental Health,* 4:255–270.

Gordon, D.A. and Young, R.D. (1976), School phobia: A discussion of aetiology, treatment and evaluation. *Psychological Reports,* 39, 783–804.

Hug-Hellmuth, H. von (1913), *Aus dem Seelenleben des Kindes*. Leipzig, Germany: Deuticke.

—— (1921), On the technique of child analysis. *International Journal of Psychoanalysis,* 2(3/4):285–305.

Johnson, A., Falstein, E., Szurek, S.A., and Svenosen, M. (1941). School phobia. *American Journal of Orthopsychiatry,* 11:702–711.

Leventhal, T. and Sills, M. (1964), Self-image in school phobia. *American Journal of Orthopsychiatry,* 34:685–695.

Prugh, D. G. (1983), *The Psychosocial Aspects of Pediatrics,* Philadelphia: Lea & Febiger, p. 582.

Schmitt, B. D. (1971), School phobia—the great imitator: A pediatrician's viewpoint. *Pediatrics,* 48:433–438.

Skynner, A. and Robin, C. (1976), *Applications of Family Techniques to the Study of a Syndrome: School Phobia,* pp. 306–328. New York: Brunner/Mazel.

Solomon, J. C. (1938). Active play therapy. *American Journal of Orthopsychiatry,* 8(3):479–498.

—— (1940), Active play therapy: further experiences. *American Journal of Orthopsychiatry,* 10(4):763–781.

—— (1951), Therapeutic use of play. In: *An Introduction to Projective Techniques,* ed. H.H. Anderson and G.L. Anderson, pp. 639–661. Englewood Cliffs, New Jersey: Prentice-Hall.

Waldfogel, S., Tessman, E., and Harhn, P. (1959), A program for early intervention in school phobia. *American Journal of Orthopsychiatry,* 29: 324–333.